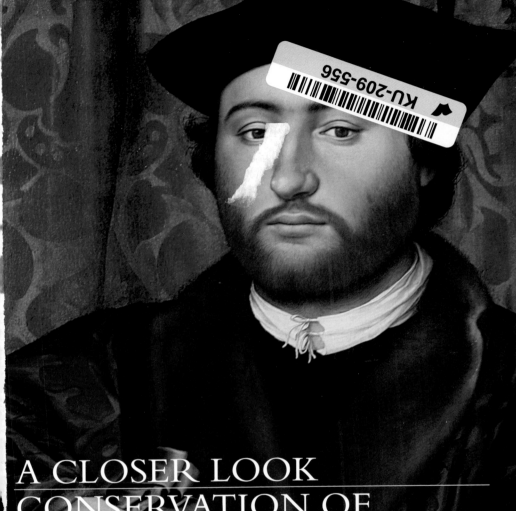

A CLOSER LOOK
CONSERVATION OF PAINTINGS

David Bomford, with Jill Dunkerton
and Martin Wyld

NATIONAL GALLERY COMPANY, LONDON
DISTRIBUTED BY YALE UNIVERSITY PRESS

David Bomford is Associate Director for Collections at the
J. Paul Getty Museum, Los Angeles. Jill Dunkerton is Restorer
and Martin Wyld is Director of Conservation at the National
Gallery, London. Jill Dunkerton co-wrote the best-selling *Giotto
to Dürer* and Martin Wyld was co-author of *Making and Meaning:
Holbein's Ambassadors.*

Take *A Closer Look* with these guides,
produced by the National Gallery, London:
Colour

Coming soon:
Faces
Frames
Saints

Front cover, half-title and title page: Hans Holbein the Younger, *Jean de
Dinteville and Georges de Selve ('The Ambassadors')*

First published in Great Britain as *Pocket Guides:
Conservation of Paintings* in 1997
Revised and expanded edition published 2009
by National Gallery Company Limited
St Vincent House, 30 Orange Street, London WC2H 7HH
ISBN 9 78185709 441 1
525551
British Library Cataloguing-in-Publication Data
A catalogue record is available from the British Library
Library of Congress Catalog Card Number: 97-67665

Written by David Bomford, with Jill Dunkerton and Martin Wyld
Pocket Guides: Conservation of Paintings, edited by Felicity Luard
and Nicola Coldstream
A Closer Look: Conservation of Paintings, edited by Claire Young
Designed by Heather Bowen
Cover designed by Smith & Gilmour
Production by Jane Hyne and Penny Le Tissier
Printed and bound in Hong Kong by Printing Express

2

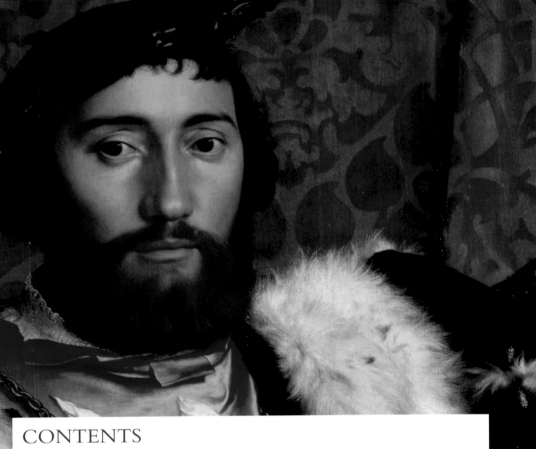

CONTENTS

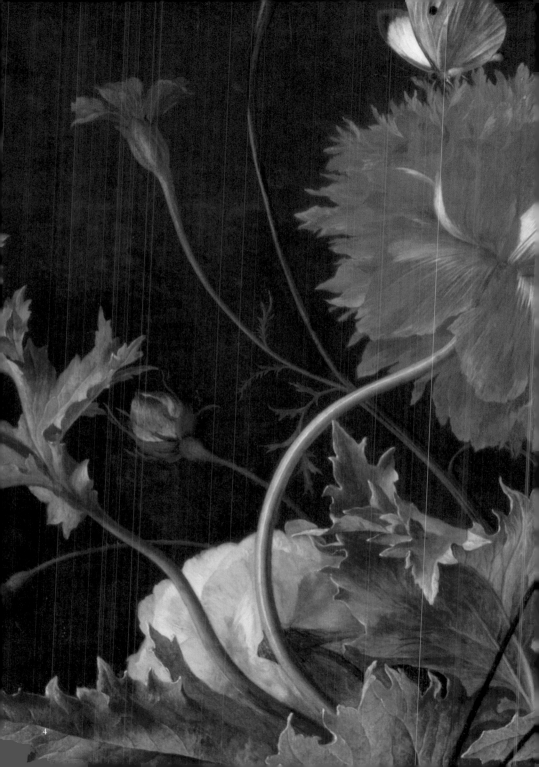

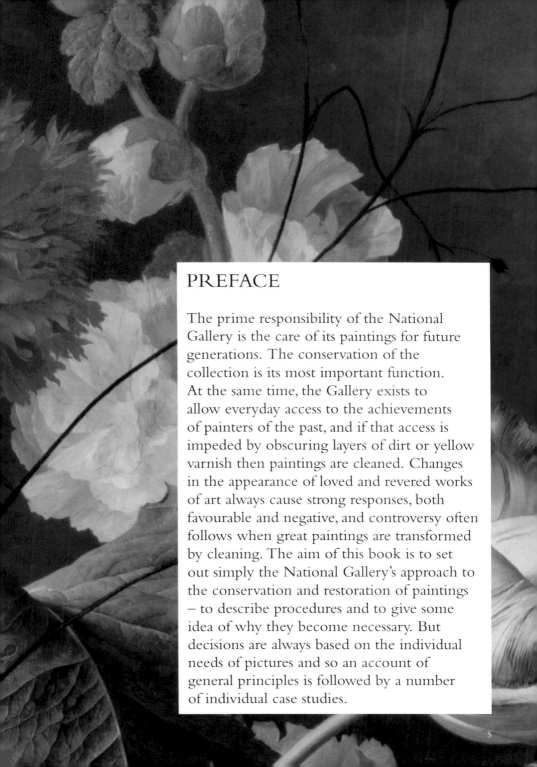

PREFACE

The prime responsibility of the National
Gallery is the care of its paintings for future
generations. The conservation of the
collection is its most important function.
At the same time, the Gallery exists to
allow everyday access to the achievements
of painters of the past, and if that access is
impeded by obscuring layers of dirt or yellow
varnish then paintings are cleaned. Changes
in the appearance of loved and revered works
of art always cause strong responses, both
favourable and negative, and controversy often
follows when great paintings are transformed
by cleaning. The aim of this book is to set
out simply the National Gallery's approach to
the conservation and restoration of paintings
– to describe procedures and to give some
idea of why they become necessary. But
decisions are always based on the individual
needs of pictures and so an account of
general principles is followed by a number
of individual case studies.

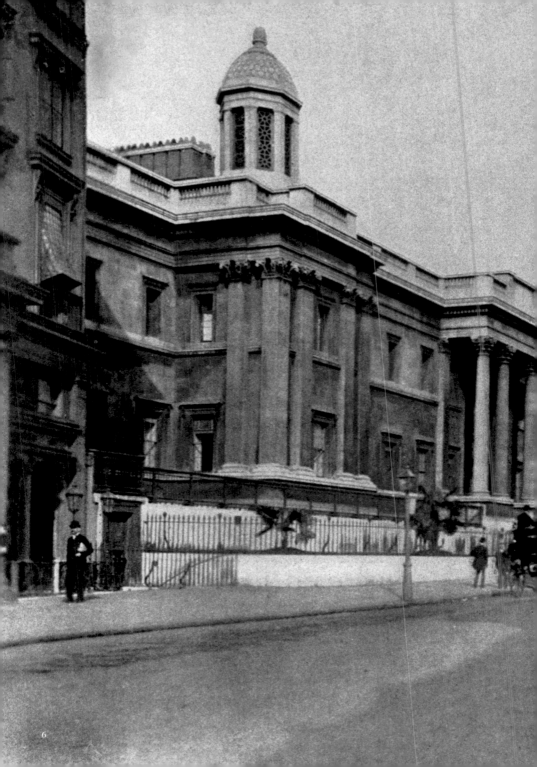

6

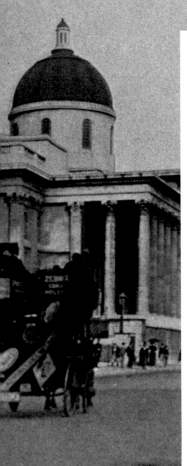

CONSERVATION IN THE PAST

The decision in the middle of the nineteenth century to locate and then to keep the National Gallery in Trafalgar Square was to have significant effects on the future conservation of the Collection. From the founding of the Gallery in temporary quarters in Pall Mall there was fierce debate about the wisdom of keeping the nation's pictures in the centre of one of the most polluted cities in the world. Serious consideration was given to removing the collection to the cleaner air of Hyde Park or Kensington Gardens, and plans were even drawn up for a grand new building close to the present site of the Royal Albert Hall, facing towards the Serpentine.

Atmospheric conditions in the centre of London, the great teeming smoky heart of Empire, are vividly conjured up in the proceedings of the various Parliamentary Select Committees that considered the question:'…the National Gallery is in the vicinity of several large chimneys, particularly those of baths, washhouses…and club-houses…and that connected with the steam-engine by which the fountains in Trafalgar Square are worked, from which great volumes of smoke are emitted…the proximity likewise of Hungerford Stairs and of that part of the Thames to which there is the constant resort of steamboats may aggravate this evil…'[3].

After long deliberation in the 1850s, the decision was made to leave the Gallery where it was, its central location being considered more important than the effects of polluted

Previous pages:

1. Detail of Jan van Huysum, *Flowers in a Terracotta Vase*, 1736–7, page 26.

2. The National Gallery, 1896

air on the paintings. A conscious choice was made for public access at the risk of possible deterioration. The significance of this choice was far-reaching, since the necessity of instituting a programme of cleaning and repair was implicit within it.

The paintings were certainly becoming exceptionally dirty. Restorations carried out in the early years of the Gallery by the first Keeper, William Seguier, and his brother, John – both picture restorers – had consisted primarily of applying coats of the notorious 'gallery varnish', a golden brown mixture of mastic and boiled linseed oil that remained tacky for a considerable time and therefore quickly became even darker in the dirty London air.

When Sir Charles Eastlake [4] became Keeper in 1844, the cleaning of paintings began in earnest. In 1846 the first five pictures freed from their brown varnishes (including Rubens's *Minerva protects Pax from Mars* ('*Peace and War*'), Cuyp's *Hilly River Landscape* and Velázquez's *Philip IV hunting Wild Boar*) were shown to an unprepared public. There was immediate outrage. In a famous letter to *The Times*, signed 'Verax', the Rubens was described as 'completely flayed...with characteristic ignorance the rich fine glazings have been scoured off'. The same 1853 Parliamentary Select Committee that considered moving the Gallery to Kensington also looked in great detail at the whole question of picture cleaning. The subsequent report – several hundred pages long – did not commit itself to a judgement on the results of the various cleanings but remarked on the conflicting opinions of 'witnesses whose fervent love of art seems to have kindled some personal animosity'.

Although Eastlake's name is nowadays largely associated with this first great cleaning controversy, he also established much that we now take for granted in modern conservation. He began the practice of keeping full conservation records for each picture in the collection – records that are still constantly referred to. He was also actively concerned with what we now call 'preventive conservation' and invited the eminent scientist Michael Faraday to collaborate in producing 'A Report on the Protection of Pictures at the National Gallery by Glass' which concluded by recommending the glazing of pictures as protection against the 'manifold evils' to which they were subjected.

Conservation and restoration of paintings continued under subsequent directors. The Gallery did not employ its own staff for such work until later and used private London restorers in long-established family firms such as those of Morrill or Holder. In 1936 another controversy flared up over the cleaning by Holder of Velázquez's *Philip IV of Spain in Brown and Silver*.

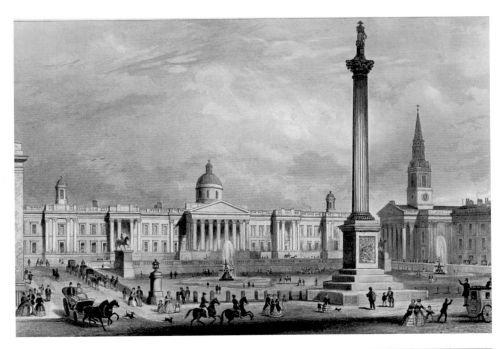

3. The National Gallery in the mid-nineteenth century.

4. Sir Charles Eastlake, Keeper, then the first Director of the National Gallery. Eastlake was appointed Director in 1855 and greatly augmented the Gallery's collection of Italian painting, making it one of the foremost in Europe.

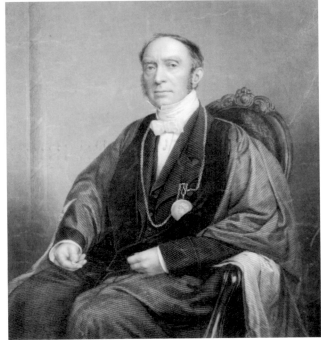

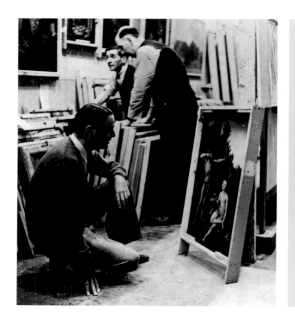

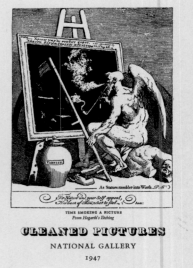

5. Sir Kenneth Clark, Director of the National Gallery 1934–45, examining a painting stored at Manod quarry, Wales. Pictures from several collections were stored here during World War II.

6. *Cleaned Pictures*, a catalogue of the 1947 exhibition.

The critic of *The Daily Telegraph* claimed that 'the beauty of the picture is seriously impaired…the patina of natural age has disappeared and, I think, the touch of the master along with it…the upper layer of the work has been destroyed.' More than fifty letters appeared in the press on the matter and the arguments continued into 1937. Nowadays the painting is considered one of the most beautifully preserved of all seventeenth-century paintings.

During World War II, when the National Gallery paintings were mostly in storage in Manod quarry, Wales [5], some 70 were cleaned by nine different restorers, including Helmut Ruhemann, formerly restorer to the Berlin museums, who had come to London in 1933 and was invited in 1934 by the Director, Sir Kenneth Clark, to be consultant restorer to the Gallery. In 1946 the paintings were seen by the public for the first time in their newly cleaned state. One hundred years and one day after Verax's letter to *The Times* of 1846, another letter to the same newspaper inaugurated a new but familiar process.

Controversy was followed this time by an explanatory exhibition of *Cleaned Pictures* [6] at the National Gallery in 1947, and then the establishment of an international commission under the chairmanship of Dr J. Weaver, which concluded that 'no damage was found to have resulted from the recent cleaning'.

The most important result of the Weaver report was to set out clear guidelines for a new Department of Conservation which

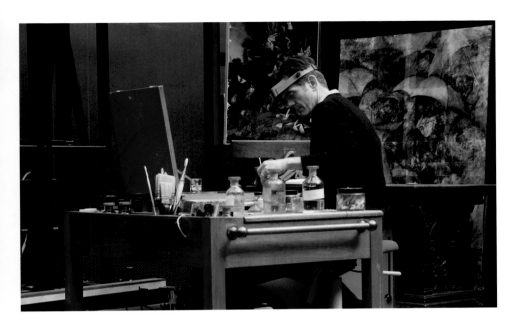

7. One of the National Gallery conservation studios today.

had been established the previous year. For the first time, the Gallery would employ its own restorers and they would work on paintings inside the building rather than in private London studios. At first, the department operated in unsatisfactory conditions in Room 9 amid constant dust from plaster loosened by war-time bombs. Later, air-conditioned studios located above the exhibition rooms were made as part of the post-war reconstruction programme and were opened in 1960 [7]. In the basement, large workshops were equipped for structural conservation – then a routine and somewhat unconsidered activity, the importance of which was to be considerably reassessed over the next three decades.

The paintings conservation department now employs nine people engaged on the practical treatment and technical examination of paintings. It works in daily collaboration with curatorial, scientific, framing, photographic and exhibition departments in maintaining, studying and displaying the collection. In recent years, research into European painting techniques has been a growing part of the department's activities – as well as continuing research into the fundamentals of conservation practice. Eastlake's belief that the conservation and restoration of paintings demand a detailed understanding of the painter's methods, materials and intentions remains central to all that the department does.

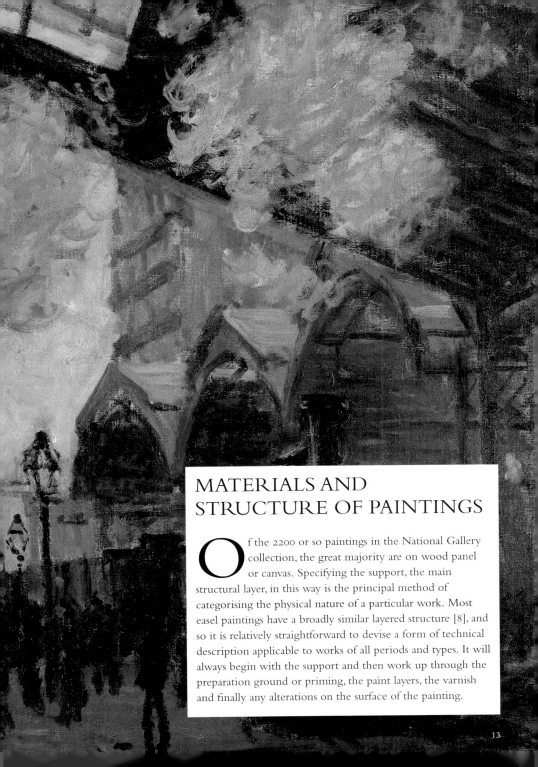

MATERIALS AND
STRUCTURE OF PAINTINGS

Of the 2200 or so paintings in the National Gallery collection, the great majority are on wood panel or canvas. Specifying the support, the main structural layer, in this way is the principal method of categorising the physical nature of a particular work. Most easel paintings have a broadly similar layered structure [8], and so it is relatively straightforward to devise a form of technical description applicable to works of all periods and types. It will always begin with the support and then work up through the preparation ground or priming, the paint layers, the varnish and finally any alterations on the surface of the painting.

CANVAS   PANEL

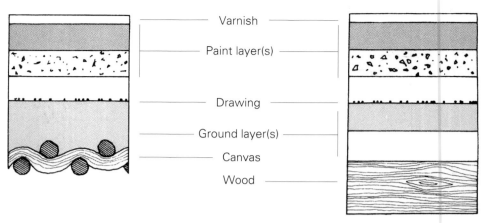

Varnish

Paint layer(s)

Drawing

Ground layer(s)

Canvas

Wood

8. Cross-sections of a prepared
and painted canvas and panel.

Wood panels for painting are usually of species typical of and
widely available in their country of origin. Early Italian paintings
are almost always on poplar, while northern European panels are
often of oak. The working methods of the original panel-makers
are sometimes visible. On the back of an untouched poplar panel
it may be possible to see the marks of tools such as the adze [9]
or, on a seventeenth-century Flemish panel, the unique guild
mark of the individual panel-maker [10]. For large panels, several
planks might be rejoined edge to edge: the great early Italian
altarpieces are made up of massive poplar planks, Holbein's
'Ambassadors' consists of 10 vertical strips of oak and Rubens's
Landscape with Het Steen comprises no fewer than 21 pieces of
oak of different shapes and sizes. Other woods used for painting
include beech, fir and even pine – despite the fact that it makes
a rather coarse and unstable support. In the eighteenth and
nineteenth centuries imported woods such as mahogany became
widely used throughout Europe.

By 'canvas' paintings we mean those on supports of fabric
stretched to keep them taut, nowadays over an expandable
wooden stretcher [11] but, before the eighteenth century, over
solid wood panels or rigid frameworks called strainers. The fabric
is usually linen – although cotton, hemp and silk are sometimes
found – and it is usually of plain weave, although the pattern
of more elaborate textures such as twill, herringbone and damask
can sometimes be seen through the paint. As with panels, it was
often necessary to join pieces together to make larger canvases
and the seams are sometimes visible.

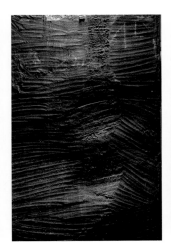
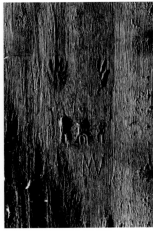

9. Original woodworking marks on the back of Carlo Crivelli's *The Vision of the Blessed Gabriele*, probably about 1489, egg tempera and oil on poplar, 141 × 87 cm. Photographed in a raking light.

10. Panel-maker's guild mark on the back of Peter Paul Rubens's *Portrait of Susanna Lunden* (?) ('*Le Chapeau de Paille*'), probably 1622–5, oil on oak, 79 × 54.6 cm.

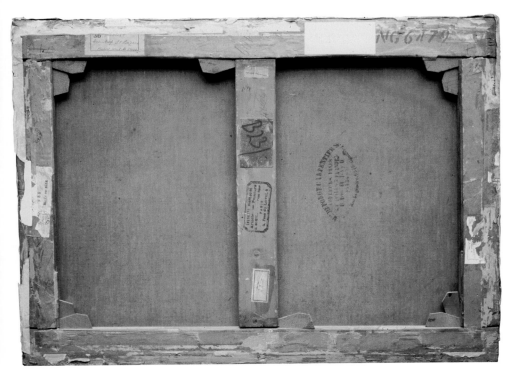

11. Back of Claude-Oscar Monet's *Gare St-Lazare*, 1877 (previous pages), oil on canvas, 54.3 × 73.6 cm, with colourman's stamp on the canvas and stretcher-maker's stamp on the centre bar.

15

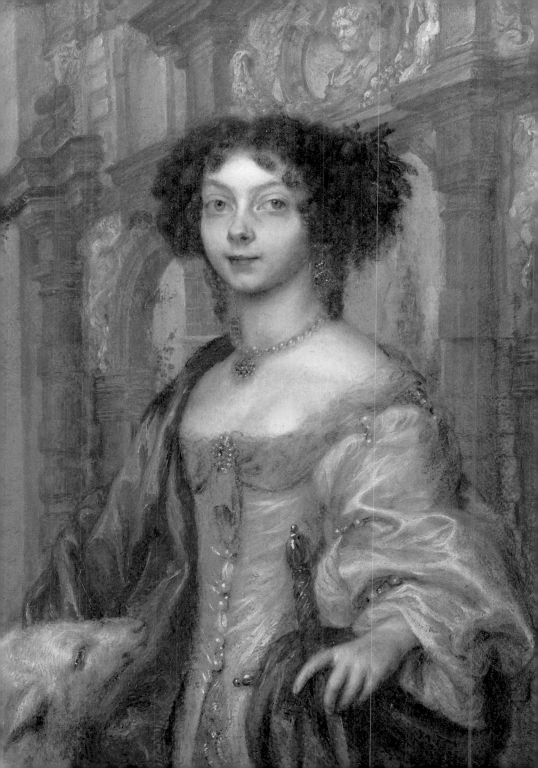

Other materials have also functioned as painting supports. Copper plates were readily available for printmaking and were quite commonly used for small, highly detailed paintings. One painting in the National Gallery is on silver, which gives it a brilliant pale tonality [12]. Vellum, slate, marble, glass, ivory, leather, tin and zinc have also been variously used for painting. In the nineteenth century, commercially prepared supports such as millboard became popular for smaller paintings and *plein-air* (outdoor) sketches.

Wood and canvas supports are, in general, unsuitable for painting on directly since they are too rough and absorbent. Traditionally they were prepared for painting with layers of ground or priming. For panels, this was usually a mixture of gypsum or chalk with animal glue, applied as a thick warm liquid and setting to a rather brittle creamy-white layer which was then scraped and rubbed smooth. For earlier Italian panels this type of ground is called *gesso* (Italian for gypsum). *Gesso* was also used for late fifteenth- and early sixteenth-century canvases, but it was soon replaced by more flexible preparations of pigments ground in oil, which became the standard form of preparation for canvases up to the twentieth century. The colour of canvas grounds could vary widely – light or dark, warm or cool, all painters had their own preferences. It was a crucial choice because it determined the tonality of the whole painting and, in many cases, it has become more dominant as the painting has aged [13].

On the ground, the painter might outline the design to be painted in some kind of underdrawing, although this stage was by no means universal. The revelation by infrared photographic techniques of spectacular underdrawings has been one of the most fascinating new developments in the study of painting techniques [14, 15].

The paint layers themselves are composed of coloured pigments mixed with a binding medium such as egg or a drying oil such as linseed oil. They can vary enormously in thickness and complexity, from thin transparent washes (glazes) to thick opaque textured brushwork (impasto). Pigments have been derived from a wide variety of sources – naturally occurring minerals (such as cinnabar, lapis lazuli, azurite and malachite), organic plant and animal products (madders, carmines, Indian yellow) or synthetic manufacture by chemical processes (lead white, lead-tin yellow, prussian blue and chrome or cadmium colours). The appearance of a painting is clearly determined by the pigments available to a painter, but the type of medium used also has a major influence on the way a paint surface looks. Oil tends to saturate pigments,

12. Gonzales Coques, *Portrait of a Woman as Saint Agnes*, about 1680, oil on silver, 18.3 × 14.4 cm. The silver support indicates that this was a highly prized portrait, perhaps of a loved one.

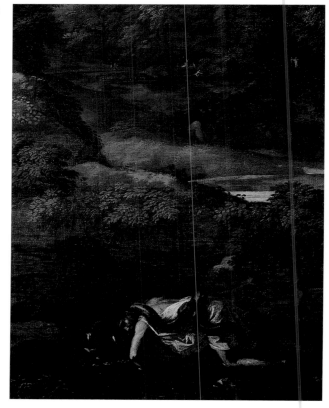

13. Nicolas Poussin, *Landscape with a Man killed by a Snake*, probably 1648, oil on canvas, 118.2 × 197.8 cm. This detail shows how the upper paint layers have become transparent over time, so that the dark red ground has become more visible. Poussin painted some of the most influential landscapes in Western art, poetic visions of nature admired by later painters such as Constable, Turner and Cézanne.

making them rich, dark and glossy, while egg leaves them less saturated, more luminous and pale.

One medium that is both optically and physically delicate is the glue (or size) that Dirk Bouts used to paint his *Entombment* in the 1450s [16]. This binder hardly wets the pigment particles at all and the paint is dry, chalky and very pale. The result is an extremely fragile and vulnerable surface – permanently water-soluble and never varnished – and it is therefore kept under protective glass.

In many paintings the paint layers are protected and the colours are given clarity and depth of saturation by a layer of clear varnish. Varnishes, consisting of natural or synthetic resins, invariably discolour with time and this is one of the reasons why pictures are cleaned. Some paintings, such as glue-tempera paintings like Bouts's *Entombment* and certain Impressionist or Cubist works, were never intended to be varnished and are irreversibly altered if they do undergo subsequent varnishing.

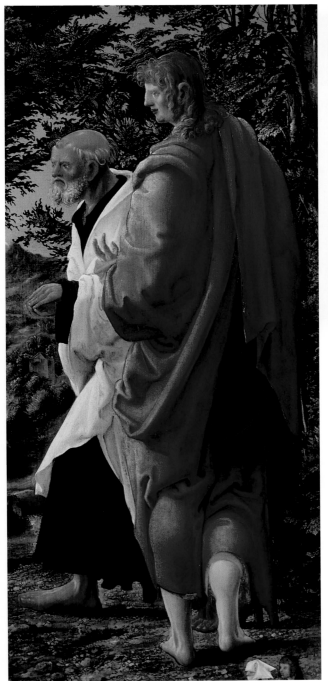

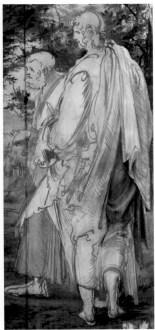

14. Albrecht Altdorfer, *Christ taking Leave of his Mother*, probably 1520, oil on lime, 141 × 111 cm. Detail of Saint John the Evangelist and the aged Saint Peter. Altdorfer spent most of his life in Regensberg, where he worked as a painter, draughtsman, designer, architect and printmaker. His skill as a draughtsman is evident in the underdrawings of his paintings.

15. Infrared reflectogram assembly of detail shown in 14, revealing the underdrawing.

16. (Next page) Dirk Bouts, *The Entombment*, probably 1450s, glue tempera on linen, 87.5 × 73.6 cm, detail. Few Netherlandish paintings of this period on linen cloth have survived. The muted and translucent colours are due to the use of a glue medium applied directly to the sized linen.

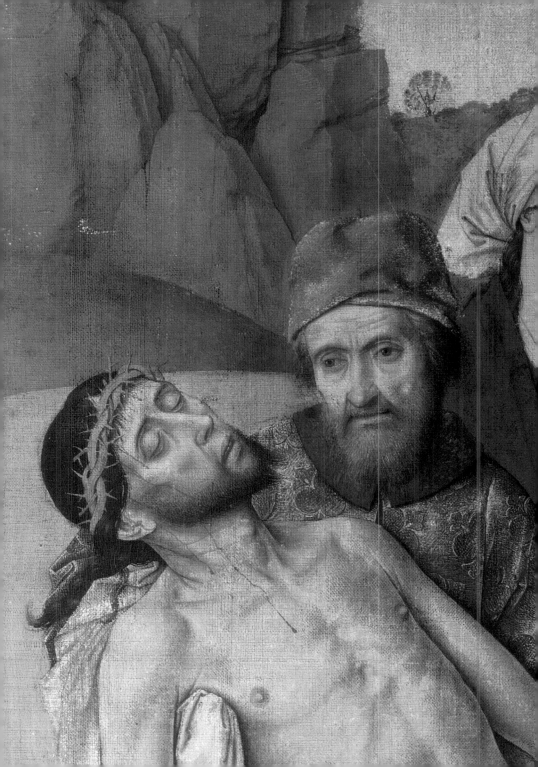

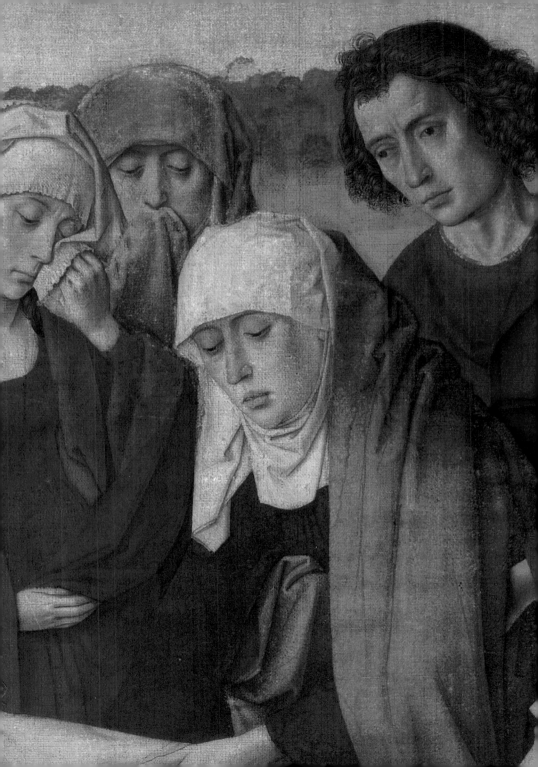

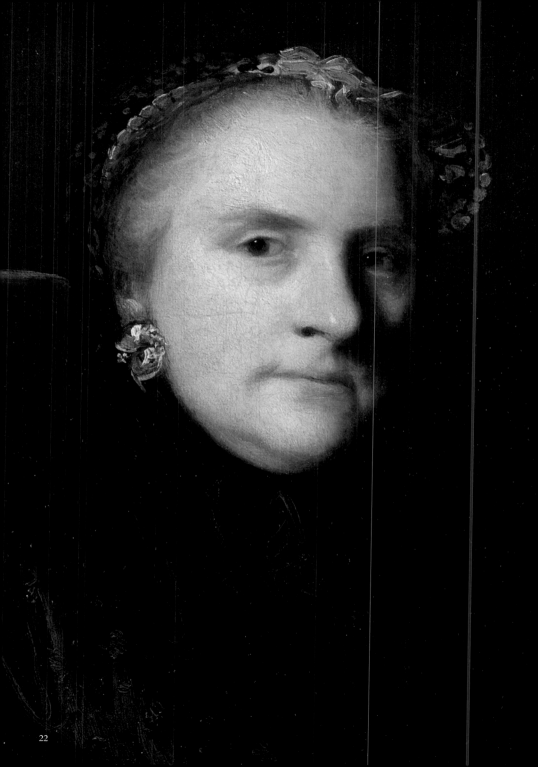

CHANGE AND DETERIORATION

All paintings begin to change from the moment the painter finishes work on them. The effects of natural ageing, light, heat and humidity, accidental damage and the sometimes necessary but frequently unwelcome attentions of owners, collectors and restorers all take their toll. Natural ageing is intrinsic to the materials of the painting. Pigments fade or change colour, the medium changes character and renders the paint more transparent, crack patterns (craquelure) develop as the paint dries, contracts and moves with the support [19]. Some of these alterations are obvious, some more subtle. In many earlier Italian paintings, the rich, green pigment copper resinate has changed under the effect of light to a deep brown or even black. A notable example is the small *Apollo and Daphne* by Antonio del Pollaiuolo [18], in which the laurel tree and the landscape have both become very dark. The fading of pigments is not uncommon.

17. (Previous pages) Sir Joshua Reynolds, *Anne, 2nd Countess of Albemarle*, about 1760, oil on canvas, 126.5 × 101 cm, detail. Reynolds was a fashionable portrait painter in eighteenth-century England. The deterioration of the flesh tones in some of Reynolds's portraits was already apparent during his lifetime, leading one wit to observe that his subjects frequently outlived their portraits.

18. Antonio del Pollaiuolo, *Apollo and Daphne*, probably 1470–80, oil on wood, 29.5 × 20 cm. The green pigment used in the foliage and landscape has darkened over time.

19. Dirk Bouts, *The Virgin and Child*, about 1465, detail, showing craquelure.

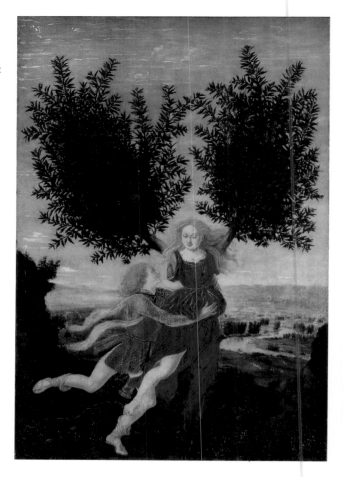

Typical examples are the deathly white complexion of Sir Joshua Reynolds's *Anne, 2nd Countess of Albemarle* [17], in which a pink tone has faded, and the blue foliage of Jan van Huysum's *Flowers in a Terracotta Vase*, from which a yellow has disappeared through the long-term effect of light [20]. Changes in the paint medium that make it more transparent allow features in the underlayers of paintings to show which were not originally intended to be seen. Often, *pentimenti* (literally, repentances), where a painter has altered part of a composition by painting over it, can become visible in this way. One clear example is the repositioned head of the young, bearded man at the left edge of Titian's *Vendramin Family* [21]. The craquelure is also a distinctive feature of many paintings. It can take two main forms: drying cracks – wide fissures caused by slow or faulty drying of the paint – and

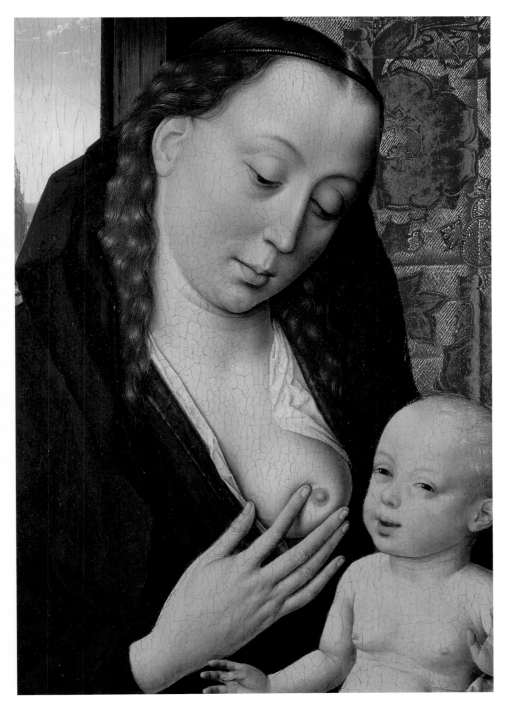

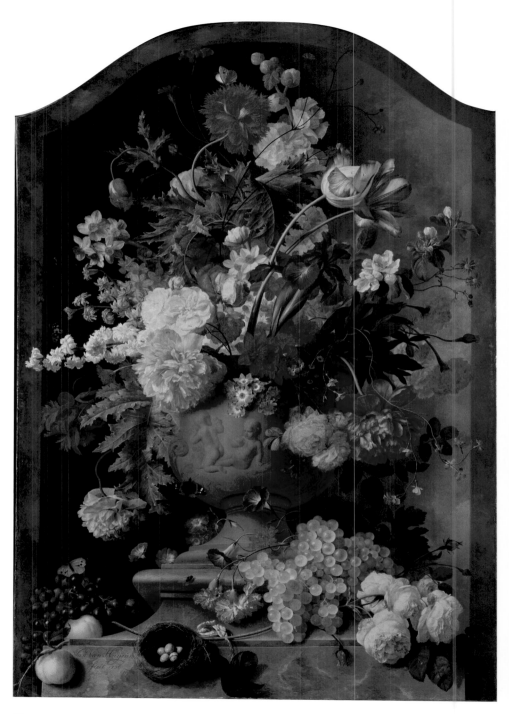

age or mechanical cracks which develop from the movement of the paint once it is hard and brittle. A notorious example of drying cracks is Reynolds's *Lord Heathfield of Gibraltar.* The painter made a number of techinical mistakes, including mixing wax and varnish resin with his oil paint. The painted surface contracted and split into rough islands as it gradually hardened [22]. The altogether more delicate web of age craquelure can be seen on many paintings in the collection.

Changes to paintings that might be described as deterioration occur because of bad hanging or storage, neglect, accident, vandalism and misguided treatment by past and present generations. Very few paintings have survived unscathed. They have usually been drawn into an inexorable cycle of damage and treatment as the centuries passed. It is now clear that much past remedial treatment by restorers – usually well-intentioned, sometimes unwise, occasionally incompetent – has contributed to the deterioration of works of art of all kinds. The modern restorer/conservator has to deal with a confused legacy of natural change, neglect, past repair and unnatural alteration, examples of which are detailed in the following pages.

20. Jan van Huysum, *Flowers in a Terracotta Vase*, 1736–7, oil on canvas, 133.5 × 91.5 cm. The leaves in this painting have turned from green to blue, as the yellow pigment has broken down over the years.

21. Titian, *The Vendramin Family*, mid-1540s, oil on canvas, 206.1 × 288.5 cm, detail. Though Titian did begin with rough sketches of his figures and other forms on the canvas, these were largely broad outlines, which he frequently re-worked and altered in the course of painting.

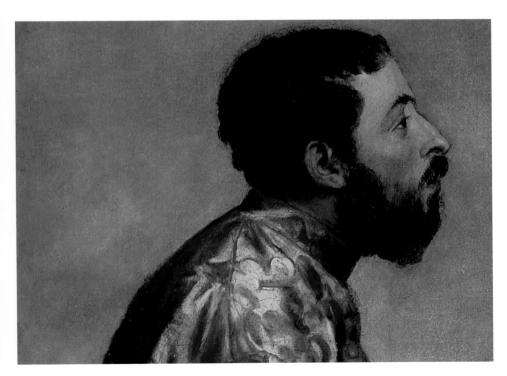

22. Sir Joshua Reynolds, *Lord Heathfield of Gibraltar*, 1787, oil on canvas, 142 × 113.5 cm, detail, showing the contracted paint surface.

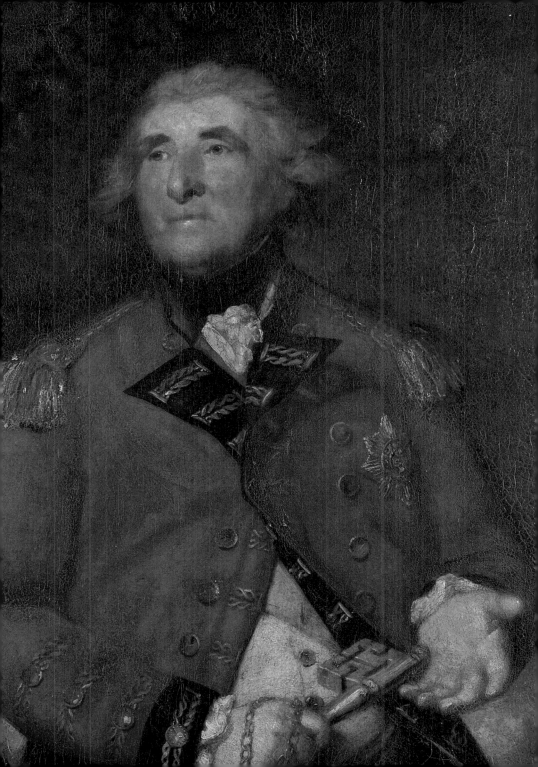

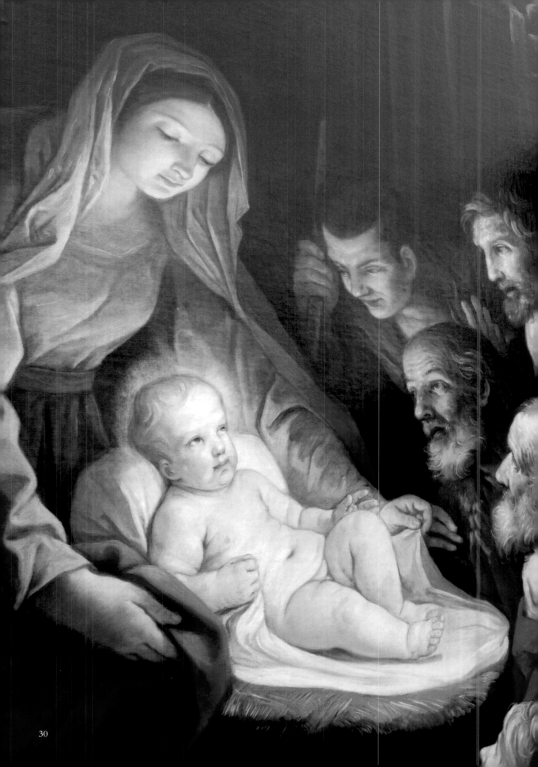

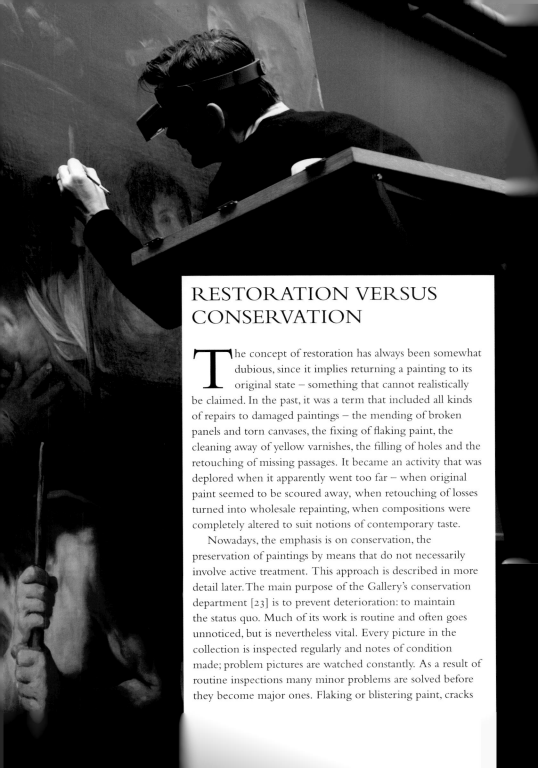

RESTORATION VERSUS CONSERVATION

The concept of restoration has always been somewhat dubious, since it implies returning a painting to its original state – something that cannot realistically be claimed. In the past, it was a term that included all kinds of repairs to damaged paintings – the mending of broken panels and torn canvases, the fixing of flaking paint, the cleaning away of yellow varnishes, the filling of holes and the retouching of missing passages. It became an activity that was deplored when it apparently went too far – when original paint seemed to be scoured away, when retouching of losses turned into wholesale repainting, when compositions were completely altered to suit notions of contemporary taste.

Nowadays, the emphasis is on conservation, the preservation of paintings by means that do not necessarily involve active treatment. This approach is described in more detail later. The main purpose of the Gallery's conservation department [23] is to prevent deterioration: to maintain the status quo. Much of its work is routine and often goes unnoticed, but is nevertheless vital. Every picture in the collection is inspected regularly and notes of condition made; problem pictures are watched constantly. As a result of routine inspections many minor problems are solved before they become major ones. Flaking or blistering paint, cracks

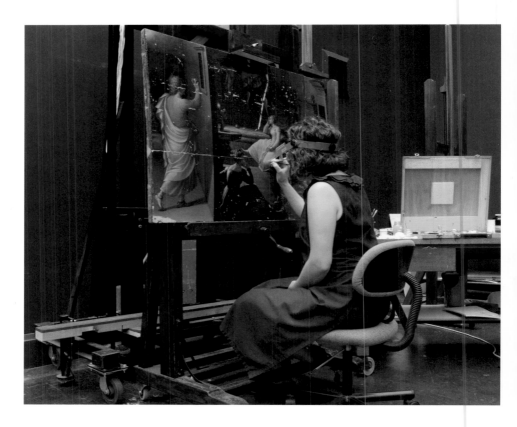

23. (Previous pages, above and top right) The conservation or restoration of paintings is undertaken at the National Gallery workshops.

24. (Below right) A minute fragment of paint, embedded in resin, is manipulated under a microscope in the National Gallery scientific department. Careful examination and observation of different parts of an artwork will inform important decisions about the care of a painting. See page 63 for a case study which features a magnified cross-section of a paint sample.

in panels and canvas distortions are examples of the type of defect that must be remedied quickly if permanent loss or damage is to be avoided. Attention to such problems is the everyday, unremarkable, essential work of the conservation department.

At the same time, paintings do become obscured by discoloured varnishes, and many still have repaints from previous restorations that conceal original paint and which can seriously mislead. Therefore a gradual programme of cleaning is being followed and it is in this specific context that we now apply the term 'restoration'. Strictly, it now means the recovery of the original paint surface from beneath varnishes and repaints and the careful retouching of missing areas. Some would define it as the latter stage alone. The processes of conservation and restoration demand a deep understanding of the original materials and processes used by painters. Much research into the fundamental materials of paintings and into conservation processes is carried out in collaboration with the National Gallery scientific department [24] and with colleagues in museums worldwide.

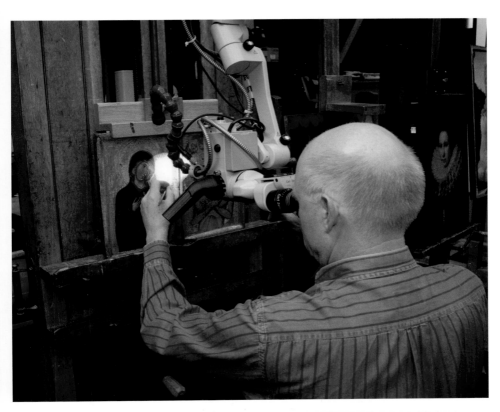

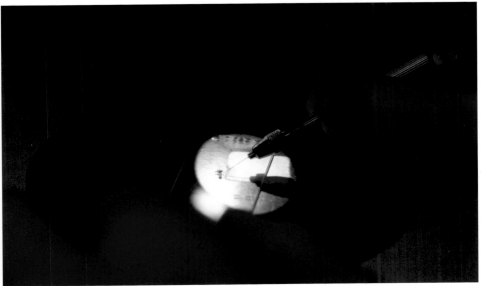

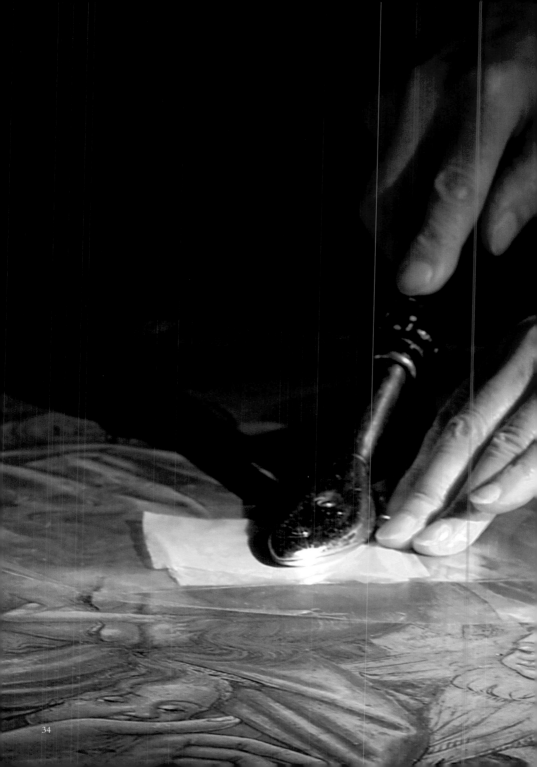

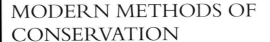

MODERN METHODS OF CONSERVATION

The main priority of present-day conservators is to ensure the long-term stability of the works of art in their care. The most important way of doing this is to control the surrounding environmental conditions, keeping light, temperature and humidity at steady levels appropriate to the types of materials the artist used. At the same time, safe methods of display and storage protect against accidental damage: for example, particularly fragile or vulnerable paintings are usually exhibited behind inconspicuous, low-reflecting glass.

These ways of preserving paintings are passive – they prevent things happening that might cause deterioration. The term preventive conservation is used to describe this sort of approach and it forms the basis of everything a modern conservator does. In an ideal world, paintings would be kept stable by 'preventive conservation' measures alone but, unfortunately, many are made of inherently unstable materials or have deteriorated in the past from neglect or mistreatment. Conservators therefore sometimes have to intervene and carry out structural treatment on paintings in order to repair or stabilise them.

The key layer of any painting, usually invisible to gallery visitors, is the support, the main structural element. Only if the support is sound can the pictorial layers remain intact. Over the years, many remedies for treating damaged or deteriorated panels and canvases have been devised, some of which were sensitive and sympathetic, some drastic and even disastrous. The modern approach is to do as little as possible: if a painting can safely be left alone, nothing is done to it. This is a quite different philosophy from that of the nineteenth or earlier twentieth centuries, when canvases and panels were routinely subjected to major structural treatments, whether or not they needed them.

Panels

The most common problems of wood panels are warping across the grain, splitting along the grain, the breaking apart of joins and the loss of paint through cracking, flaking and blistering. As ever, these problems are often compounded by treatments carried out by previous generations of restorers.

Warping is caused by the fact that the back of a panel gains and loses moisture more readily than the front, which is sealed by the paint layers. Repeated swelling and shrinkage of the exposed wood can lead to a permanent compression of the wood cells on the back face and the consequent warping of the panel with the paint on the convex side. This can be corrected temporarily by exposure of the back to high humidity, but will recur as the latter dries out. Nowadays, slightly curved panels are considered acceptable but in the past fierce restraints were applied in order to keep them flat and these have done a great deal of harm. Heavy wood or metal battens were often attached to the back of a panel [26], but as it tried to move with fluctuating humidity it would strain against the much stronger battens and break apart – either at a join or, more seriously, along a weakness in the wood grain.

Even worse were the practices of thinning (reducing the thickness of a panel by shaving away wood from the back) and cradling. A cradle is a grid-like framework consisting of fixed bars glued to the back of the panel parallel to the wood grain, with free-running cross-pieces passing through slots cut in them. In theory, the panel can expand or contract across the grain while the warp is controlled but, in practice, the cross-pieces often become jammed. The panel is then liable to corrugate and crack along the line of each fixed bar, especially if – as is often the case – it was thinned before the cradle was applied. The paradox of this type of treatment is that, if a cradle functions correctly, the panel was probably strong and stable enough not to need it in the first place.

Present-day practice is to leave panels as unrestrained as possible. Where battens or cradles are not actually causing harm they can be left alone but, if there is obvious strain in the panel, they are removed by careful sawing and chipping with sharp chisels [27]. If a panel is strong enough to support itself, it can simply be framed and displayed as it is, but for weak panels, perhaps weakened further by past thinning, some kind of secondary support is necessary. Commonly these days this takes the form of a tray, a cushioned backboard which holds the panel unobtrusively at the edges with flexible pads: this system allows

25. (Previous pages) A conservator re-attaches loose paint using a heated spatula.

26. Wooden battens formerly attached to the back of Francesco Botticini's *Assumption of the Virgin*, probably about 1475–6, tempera on wood, 228.6 × 377.2 cm.

27. Removal of a cradle.

28. (Next page) A panel-joining table.

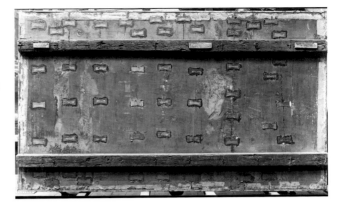

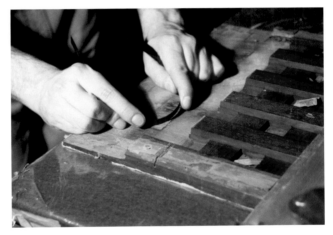

movement and at the same time protects the back of the panel from sudden fluctuations in humidity.

The mending of splits or joins that have come apart is sometimes necessary. Occasionally, badly mended joins might have to be re-broken to align them properly. To help with accurate alignment of splits and joins, a panel-joining table [28] is used by Gallery conservators: this provides horizontal pressure on the edges of the panel to push the sides of the split or join together while the adhesive is setting, together with vertical pressure from above and below to keep both sides in register.

One of the most common problems of panel paintings (and of canvas paintings too) is flaking or blistering paint caused by movement of the support. Re-attachment of loose paint using adhesives and heated spatulas is a routine operation in any conservation studio [25].

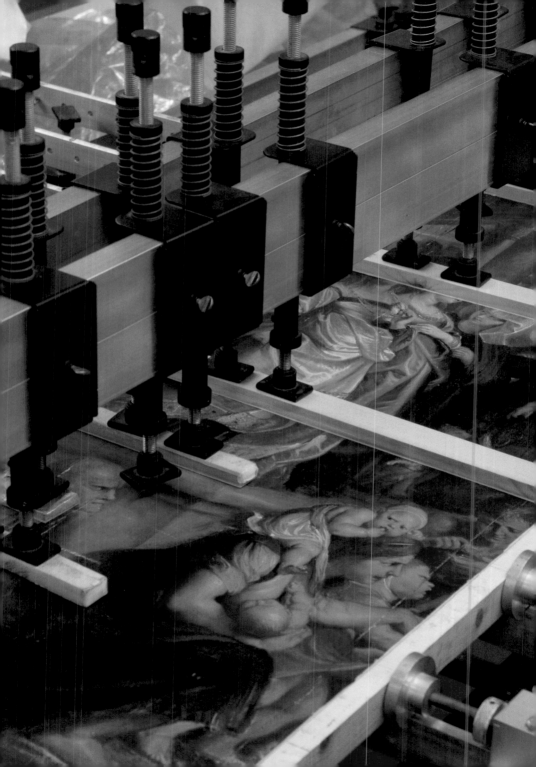

Canvases

Canvas is a more vulnerable support than wood, easily torn or dented by impact, and also sensitive to humidity, sagging or tightening as the weather changes. As it ages, it becomes more fragile as the fibres lose their flexibility and in extreme cases can even disintegrate.

To deal with torn, distorted or simply weak canvases, the standard treatment has been – and often still is – lining, in which the painting is taken off its stretcher, mounted on a second canvas and then re-stretched. This process of reinforcement gives strength, corrects distortions and sticks down the edges of tears and holes. Moreover, the adhesive used to attach the new lining can be made to penetrate through the original canvas to secure any flaking paint from behind. When a first lining eventually in its turn becomes old and perished it is taken off and replaced with a new one – the process of relining. The traditional method of attaching a lining was to use animal glues and hot tailors' irons.

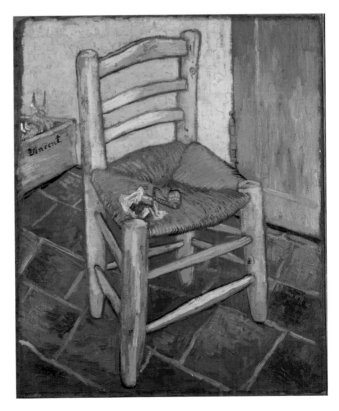

29. Vincent van Gogh, *Van Gogh's Chair*, 1888, oil on canvas, 91.8 × 73 cm. This detail shows exposed canvas around edges darkened by wax lining.

Expertly done, this alarming technique could achieve satisfactory results. However, the old methods could also do much harm by scorching, crushing and scraping the paint layers. A good deal of the damage to paintings uncovered by today's restorers and blamed on over-cleaning was, in fact, caused by past liners and subsequently concealed by repaint and discoloured varnish.

Another problematic aspect of lining is the choice of adhesive. Whereas water-based animal glues worked well for most paintings, occasionally and unpredictably they would cause disastrous shrinkage of the canvas. To avoid this, wax-based adhesives were introduced as a safer alternative: however, they were less effective at correcting deformations in paint and canvas and had the added disadvantage of severely darkening some types of painting [29].

In the past, the lining of canvas paintings was an almost automatic stage in the restoration process – whether or not it was necessary. Very few pre-nineteenth-century paintings have escaped. Works in the National Gallery Collection that have remained unlined include Moroni's *Canon Ludovico di Terzi*, *The Brazen Serpent* [30] and *Moses striking the Rock* by Giaquinto, and Velázquez's *Philip IV of Spain in Brown and Silver* [31]. The freshness and precision of their paint surfaces

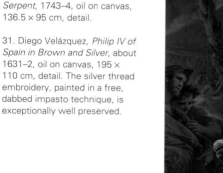

30. Corrado Giaquinto, *The Brazen Serpent*, 1743–4, oil on canvas, 136.5 × 95 cm, detail.

31. Diego Velázquez, *Philip IV of Spain in Brown and Silver*, about 1631–2, oil on canvas, 195 × 110 cm, detail. The silver thread embroidery, painted in a free, dabbed impasto technique, is exceptionally well preserved.

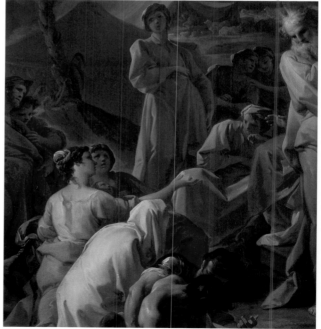

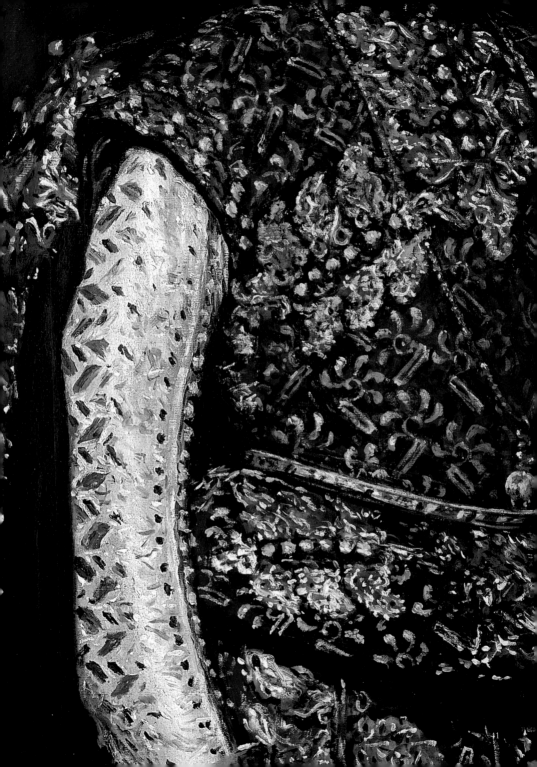

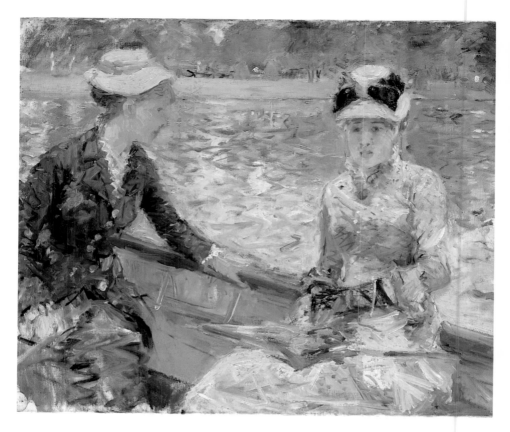

32. Berthe Morisot, *Summer's Day*, about 1879, oil on canvas, 45.7 × 75.2 cm, detail. Morisot moved to Paris in about 1852 where she met Jean-Baptiste-Camille Corot, one of the most successful and versatile nineteenth-century landscape painters, who became her most important mentor. Morisot came to know a number of the Impressionists, and later participated in their exhibitions. She painted landscapes and scenes of modern life, working in oils, pastels and watercolours.

is striking. A number of nineteenth-century paintings, including key Impressionist works such as Monet's *Gare St-Lazare* (pages 12–13), Renoir's *At the Theatre* and Morisot's *Summer's Day* [32] are also unlined. Nowadays the integrity and undisturbed textures of unlined paintings are much prized and the unnecessary and indiscriminate lining of many paintings is a cause for regret. Especially serious was the wax treatment of many Impressionist and Cubist works in collections all over the world, their dry, pale tonalities now irretrievably darkened, their delicate opacity now greasy and transparent.

Despite all these reservations, lining is still occasionally required – for example, in the case of badly torn paintings – and relining of previously lined but now deteriorated canvases is sometimes inevitable. In some studios it is still carried out safely by highly skilled practitioners using hand-irons but, increasingly, low-pressure suction tables such as that in use here at the Gallery are employed [33]. A painting is held by gentle suction against

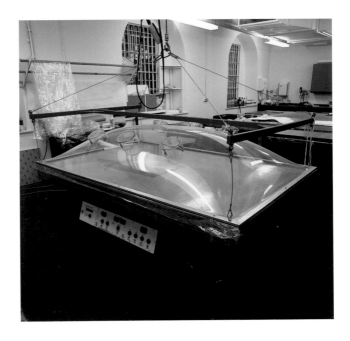

33. Low-pressure suction table developed by the National Gallery. The dome permits the controlled introduction of small amounts of humidity.

the minutely perforated surface while precise applications of heat, humidity and pressure are made, either to the whole canvas or to small areas. The control possible with tables such as these and the availability of new formulations of lining adhesive allows the attachment of linings with minimal pressure and virtually no penetration of adhesive: canvases can, therefore, be reinforced where necessary without any of the drawbacks of traditional methods.

Lining used to be the universal panacea for any defect found in canvas paintings but, in tune with the present-day philosophy of minimal intervention, they are now treated only for what is actually wrong with them. Many canvases can be treated without lining. Dents or distortions can be collected by gentle pressure with controlled heat and humidity. Small holes and tears and weak tacking edges (the margins of the canvas turned around, and tacked to the stretcher edges), which tear away from the stretcher, are strengthened with almost invisible gossamer-like fabrics. Flaking paint can be treated locally by the standard methods of blister treatment used for panels. The suction table is particularly useful for introducing small quantities of adhesive into fragile paint surfaces: one such treatment that would have been impossible by any other method was the painstaking consolidation of Van Gogh's exceptionally delicate unlined *Wheatfield, with Cypresses* (pages 70–3).

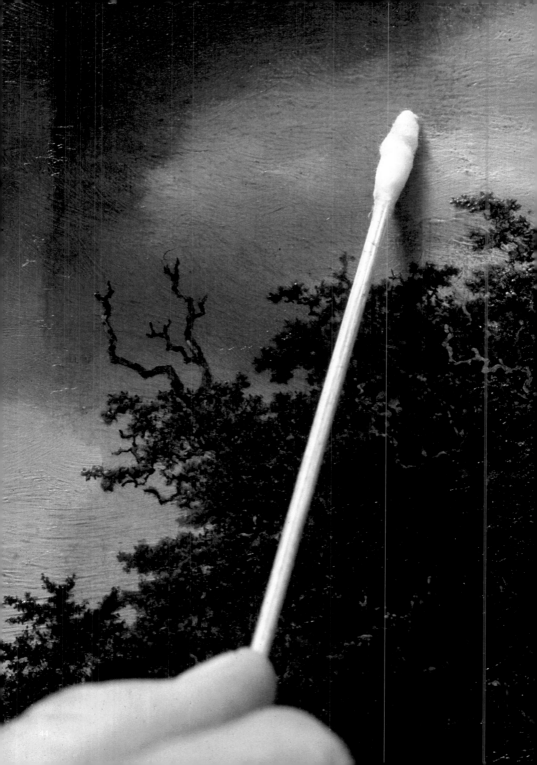

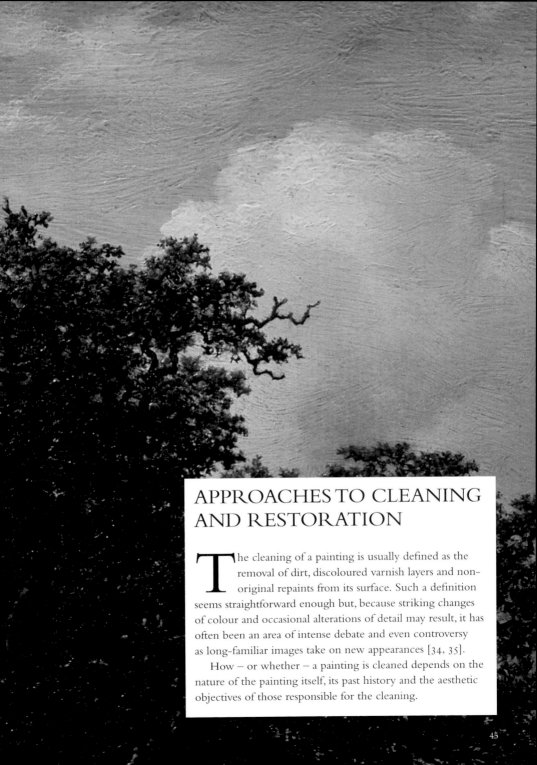

APPROACHES TO CLEANING AND RESTORATION

The cleaning of a painting is usually defined as the removal of dirt, discoloured varnish layers and non-original repaints from its surface. Such a definition seems straightforward enough but, because striking changes of colour and occasional alterations of detail may result, it has often been an area of intense debate and even controversy as long-familiar images take on new appearances [34, 35].

How – or whether – a painting is cleaned depends on the nature of the painting itself, its past history and the aesthetic objectives of those responsible for the cleaning.

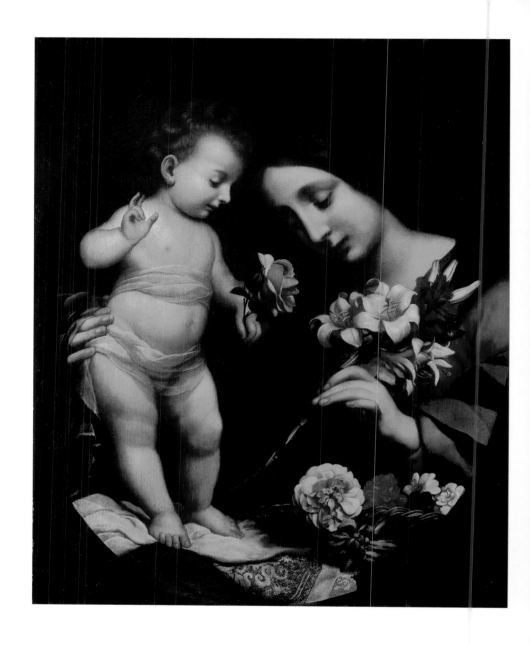

34. After Carlo Dolci, *The Virgin and Child with Flowers*, after 1642, oil on canvas. 78.1 × 63.2 cm, before cleaning.

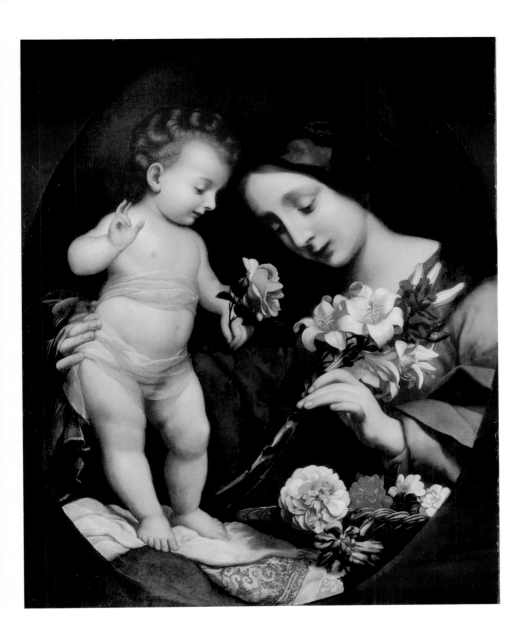

35. 34, after cleaning.

As with conservation treatments, every case is examined individually and a unique assessment made of condition and the likely consequences of cleaning. Before any treatment proceeds, a balanced appraisal of the advantages and disadvantages is made by curators and restorers, informed where necessary by the results of technical examination. Is cleaning necessary? Can it be done safely? Is the painting too damaged under those layers of repaint? Is it better to preserve the restoration of the past than to attempt our own? Such questions as these are always discussed. The final decision is made by the Trustees of the National Gallery on the advice of the Director and, in some cases, it is decided that cleaning should not be attempted.

Cleaning might be ruled out for a variety of reasons. For some paintings that were extensively damaged and repainted in previous centuries, cleaning could result in a severely fragmented image that is, in its way, as misleading as the restoration that now conceals it. Gentile Bellini's *Sultan Mehmet II* [45] is a notable example of a famous image too damaged to clean and Pisanello's *Virgin and Child with Saint George and Saint Anthony Abbot* [47] is of uncertain status, having been recorded, while in Eastlake's collection, as 'rubbed to the ground' in places and repainted for him by the Milanese restorer Giuseppe Molteni.

Other paintings cannot be cleaned for technical reasons. Some artists incorporated waxes or resins into their paints which might be soluble in the kinds of solvents used for cleaning. In the eighteenth and nineteenth centuries especially, the abandonment of traditional workshop practice led to experimentation with unstable and impermanent artists' materials which can make cleaning hazardous, if not impossible. Some of the panels of George Stubbs [52] were painted in a soapy wax medium, still soluble in the mildest of cleaning solvents.

When cleaning is decided upon, it can proceed through several stages. First, accumulations of grey dirt and grime are removed from the surface. Even this simple procedure can result in a spectacular recovery of the original colours, such as that seen in the tiny *'Vision of a Knight'* by Raphael [37], or the large *Bathers at Asnières* by Georges Seurat [38]. Removal of surface dirt may be all that is required. Usually, however, there are layers of resin varnish that have discoloured, leading to an overall yellowing and darkening of the image. In the nineteenth and early twentieth centuries, artificial toning was sometimes incorporated to give varnishes the 'golden glow' that was then so much admired. There may also be dirt between successive varnish layers if the painting has been revarnished more than once.

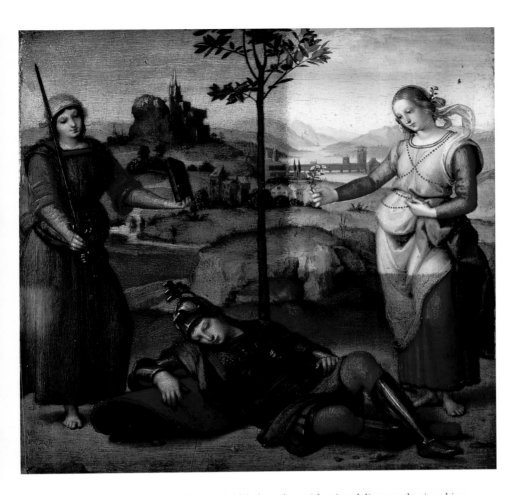

36. (Pages 44–5) Cleaning
in progress.

37. Raphael, *An Allegory
('Vision of a Knight')*, about 1504,
oil on poplar, 17.1 × 17.3 cm.
The dirt layer has been partly
removed, revealing Raphael's
skilled coupling of harmonious
colours in the personification
of Pleasure's draperies.

38. (Next page) Georges Seurat,
Bathers at Asnières, 1884, oil
on canvas, 201 × 300 cm. This
cleaning, which was undertaken
in 1971, revealed the freshness
of Seurat's palette.

Removal of darkened varnishes is a delicate and painstaking
process, carried out with small amounts of solvent on cotton
wool swabs [36]. Clearly, it is an operation that cannot allow the
smallest margin of error. The solvents chosen must be capable
of softening the varnish but not the original paint. Solvent theory
has shown that there is a small group of volatile solvents that will
readily dissolve natural resin varnishes but not dried oil paint,
and these are the materials that are generally used for cleaning
paintings. Nevertheless, constant examination on a microscopic
scale is necessary to be aware of variations in the painter's
technique that might require a cleaning method to be modified.
In the past, the use of abrasive cleaners, powerful solvents or
strong chemical reagents has commonly caused the erosion
of some paint surfaces, leaving them thin and worn. It is now

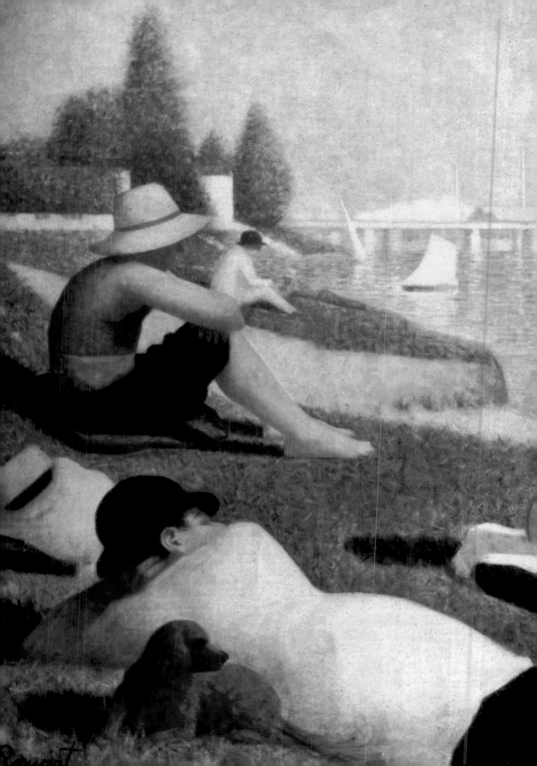

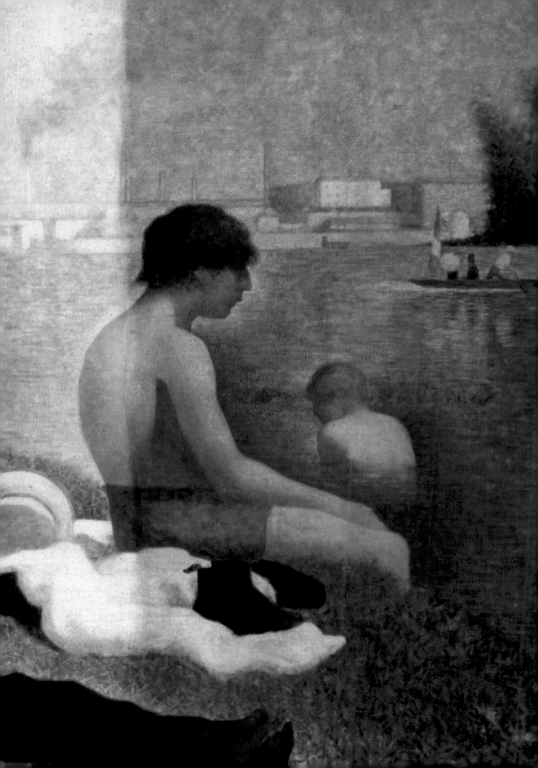

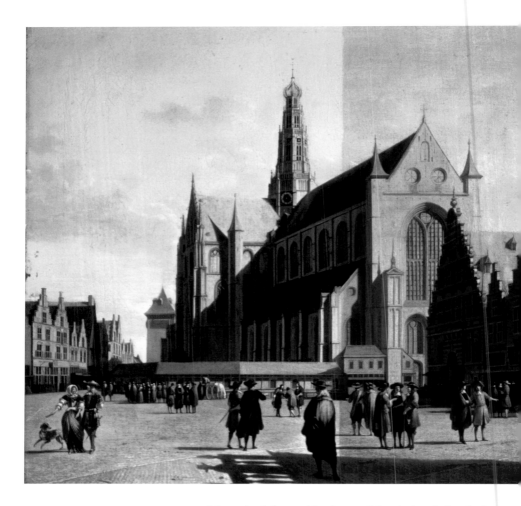

possible to check, by sensitive forms of chemical analysis, whether the vulnerable components of a paint film remain intact through the cleaning process. Cleaning does not proceed if there is any danger of removing original material. Discoloured varnishes affect the colours of a painting unevenly. Because they are generally yellowish-brown, they reinforce warm tones but counteract cooler blues, greens and whites. Moreover, they are often slightly cloudy and this has the effect of not only darkening the lights but also lightening the darks, diminishing the tonal range of a painting. Removal of old varnishes, therefore, can have a dramatic effect on the overall colour, balance and depth of a composition [39]. In some cases, even the presence of a clear varnish can distort the painter's original intentions: the Impressionists and

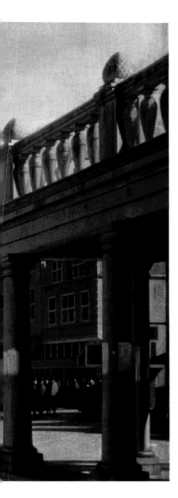

39. Gerrit Berckheyde, *The Market Place and the Grote Kerk at Haarlem*, 1674, oil on canvas, 51.8 × 67 cm. Canvas partly cleaned, revealing the artist's skilled handling of light and spatial recession. Berckheyde was born in Haarlem, where he trained under his brother Job and Frans Hals. This view must have been a particular favourite as he painted several versions.

Cubists often chose to leave the surfaces of their paintings dry and unsaturated and, unfortunately, many of their works have been irreversibly changed by later varnishing.

Varnish removal may not complete the cleaning process, since paintings have often been retouched to conceal past damages and losses or repainted in parts to alter the composition. The conservator must then distinguish between original and non-original material and arrive at a rational judgement about whether to remove some or all of the later paint. This may be done with the same solvents used for varnish removal or may require gentle scraping with scalpels under a microscope. It is usually worthwhile removing old retouchings since they often cover large amounts of perfectly well-preserved paint around the damages they were put on to conceal.

Cleaning may involve all these stages but it is important to realise that there is no absolute level to which a painting has to be cleaned. Quite different degrees of dirt, varnish and repaint removal may be appropriate for different paintings. Although cleaning is sometimes necessary for the purposes of conservation treatment, it is undertaken primarily for aesthetic reasons and different aesthetic decisions can be equally valid as long as they can be achieved safely – but, of course, the end results may look very different. As the Italian restorer Cesare Brandi wrote 40 years ago, 'every cleaning is an act of critical interpretation'.

Nevertheless, in many instances it is possible and desirable to proceed through all the stages of cleaning and reveal unobscured original paint. A cleaned painting can be in almost perfect condition, or can look distinctly alarming with all its old damages showing [40]. Paint may also be original but not have its original appearance: pigments may have changed colour or faded, or increased transparency of the paint may reveal underlayers not originally visible.

The conservator then has another aesthetic decision to make: how much restoration should be done – that is, how much of the old damage should be concealed by new retouching? Cleaning decisions certainly determine the way a painting looks, but so too does the approach to restoration. Restoration has to balance two conflicting requirements – those of legibility and authenticity. On the one hand, an observer wishes to see a composition uninterrupted by damage and loss; but, on the other, it is necessary to know which parts are original paint and which are not. These two requirements are usually satisfied by insisting on a full photographic record of the true condition of a cleaned work, followed by restoration. All restoration is a compromise,

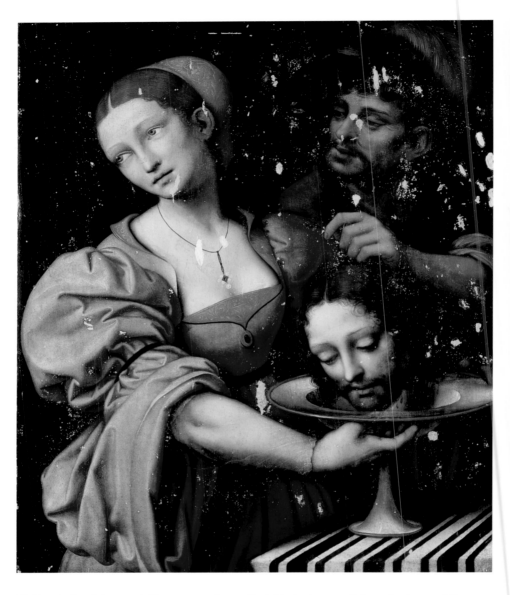

40. Giampietrino, *Salome*, probably about 1510–30, oil on poplar, 68.6 × 57.2 cm, after cleaning and before restoration.

attempting to diminish the impact of disruptive losses while allowing a painting to appear gracefully old. For example, craquelure, a signifier of age, is not normally retouched: we expect an old paint film to be cracked and it is not usually disturbing. Only where wide, white shrinkage cracks arise from a technical failure of the paint medium might a small amount of retouching be acceptable [41, 43].

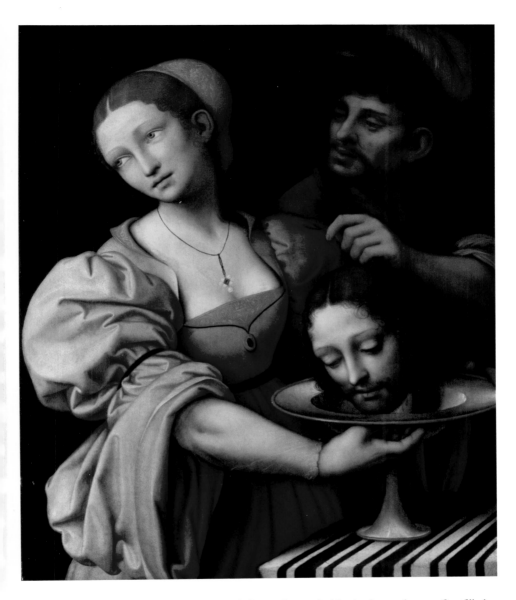

41. 40, after restoration.

If it is decided to make good old paint losses, they are first filled with a putty, textured to match the surrounding paint surface. Retouching (or inpainting) is then carried out over the filling, taking care not to encroach on to the adjacent original paint. Normally the attempt is made to reconstruct as fully as possible the missing parts of a composition within the outlines of the damage – continuing the design and matching colours

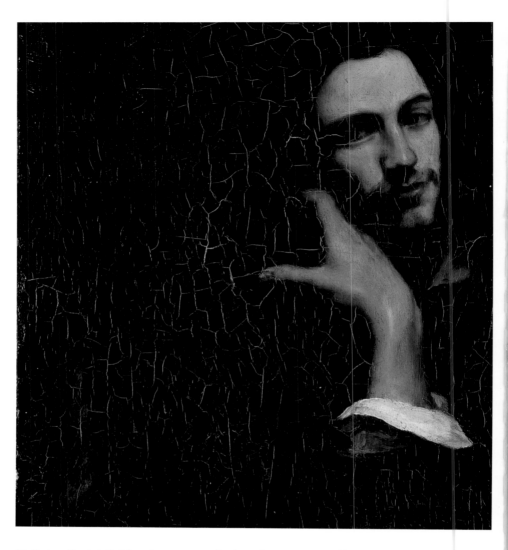

42. Gustave Courbet, *Self Portrait (L'Homme à la Ceinture de Cuir)*, 1845–50, oil on board, 45 × 37.8 cm, detail. After cleaning, before restoration. Courbet, the self-proclaimed 'proudest and most arrogant man in France', painted about 20 self portraits between 1842 and 1855 in which he assumed a range of personae; from a musician to a wounded lover to a man driven to the edge of sanity.

as completely as these can reasonably be inferred [42]. If, however, it is not possible or not thought appropriate to carry out deceptive retouching, then some sort of visually distinct inpainting can be done. This could be a single unobtrusive colour (a so-called 'neutral tone') or a partial reconstruction in which the pattern of the retouching is left plainly evident. Three panels from Duccio's 'Maestà' in the National Gallery Collection demonstrate some forms of visible retouching (pages 80–3).

Whatever type of retouching is chosen, the new paint used should be stable, should discolour as little as possible and

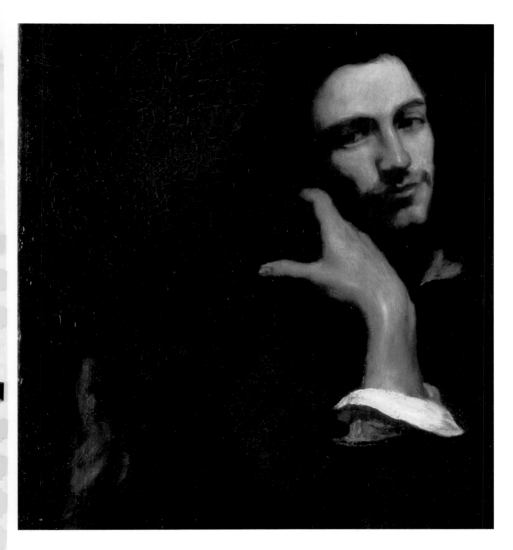

43. 42, after cleaning and restoration.

should remain easily removable in solvents that will not affect the original paint. In practice, either watercolours or synthetic resin paints are used; oil paint is not satisfactory for inpainting as it discolours and becomes very hard. The final stage of the restoration is to apply a clear varnish over the painting – except, of course, in those cases where the surface should be left unvarnished. A picture varnish should be stable and reversible, ensuring that cleaning will not need to be repeated for a long time and that, if it does eventually become necessary, it can be achieved with the least possible intervention.

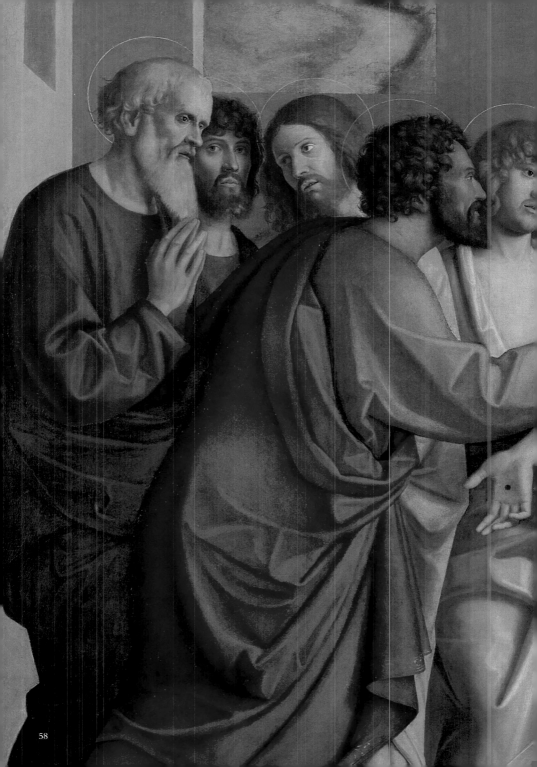

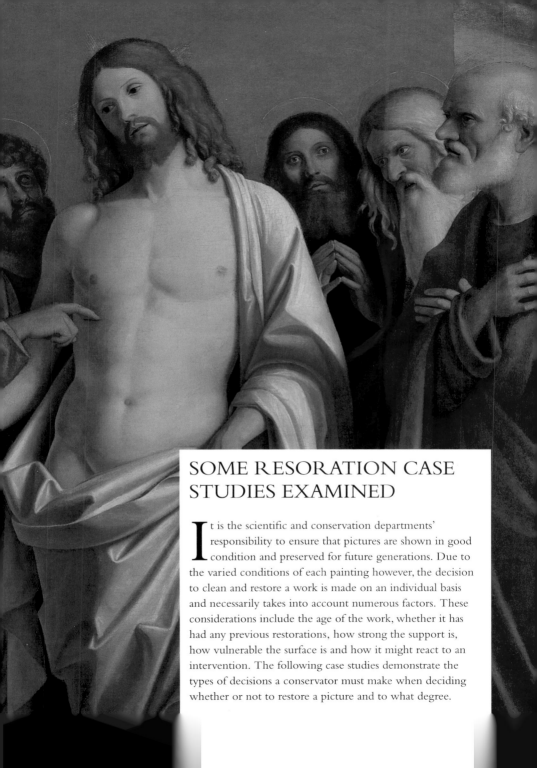

SOME RESORATION CASE STUDIES EXAMINED

It is the scientific and conservation departments'
responsibility to ensure that pictures are shown in good
condition and preserved for future generations. Due to
the varied conditions of each painting however, the decision
to clean and restore a work is made on an individual basis
and necessarily takes into account numerous factors. These
considerations include the age of the work, whether it has
had any previous restorations, how strong the support is,
how vulnerable the surface is and how it might react to an
intervention. The following case studies demonstrate the
types of decisions a conservator must make when deciding
whether or not to restore a picture and to what degree.

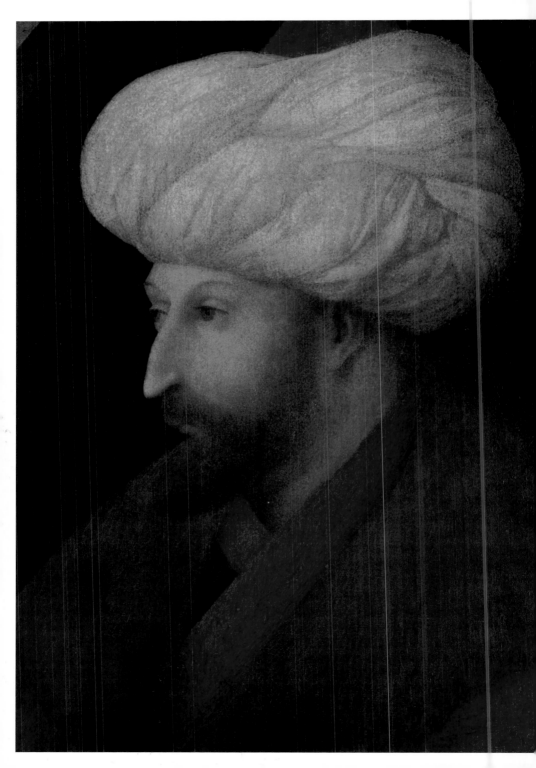

CASE STUDY 1:
DAMAGE
CONCEALED

Attributed to Gentile Bellini,
The Sultan Mehmet II, 1480
Pisanello, *The Virgin and Child with Saints*,
about 1435–41

These two works were acquired within a few
years of each other and were restored in Italy
by the same celebrated restorer in the 1850s
and 1860s.

The Bellini [45] was bought in somewhat
obscure circumstances from an old man, said to
be the son of an Englishman, in Venice in 1865,
by Layard of Nineveh for just £5. The Pisanello
was bought by Eastlake from the Costabili
collection in Ferrara in 1858. In his diary
Eastlake noted its condition – the sky 'almost
rubbed to the ground' and the armour and dress
of Saint George 'once beautifully finished but
now almost totally obliterated' – and kept it for
his personal collection as he considered it too
damaged to purchase for the National Gallery.
Ultimately it found its way into the collection
anyway, since it was presented by Lady Eastlake
in her husband's memory in 1867.

The paintings were restored by Giuseppe
Molteni, *conservatore* at the Brera, Milan, and
Eastlake's preferred restorer abroad. Molteni
worked on a number of paintings bought
for the Gallery in Italy and, in recent years,
investigations of the paintings themselves
together with archival evidence have revealed
the extent of his 'restorations' on damaged and
undamaged pictures alike. It was said of him that
he took part in 'the battle to correct the naive
inaccuracies of the old masters' and he certainly
reworked compositions to conform to his own
notions of decorum. We can judge the extent

44. (Previous pages) Detail of Giovanni Battista
Cima da Conegliano, *The Incredulity of Saint
Thomas*, about 1502–4, see pages 74–5.

45. (Opposite) Attributed to Gentile Bellini, *The
Sultan Mehmet II*, 1480, oil (nineteenth-century
repaint) on canvas, perhaps transferred from
wood, 69.9 × 52.1 cm. Gentile Bellini visited
Constantinople in 1479–81, where he painted
this work.

46. X-ray of 45.

of his work on *Sultan Mehmet II* from a modern
X-ray [46], which shows that, under Molteni's
repaint, the original painting is a ruin, with large
pieces of canvas missing and much of the paint
flaked away. The paint that we can see is all
Molteni's and as an historical likeness it is almost
wholly untrustworthy. Although the restoration
and the varnish have darkened, there is no
question of cleaning it, since only fragments
of the original survive.

The true state of Pisanello's painting [47] is
more difficult to judge, but examination under
the microscope reveals that Molteni repainted
it substantially and that much of the present

finish of the picture is due to him. Indeed, so pleased was Molteni with his work on it that he spoke (jokingly we might guess) of changing his first name from Giuseppe to Vittore, then thought to be Pisanello's. Molteni's paint seems to follow the original design fairly closely; investigations to determine the exact condition of the authentic painting that underlies this famous image will continue but cleaning is not at present contemplated.

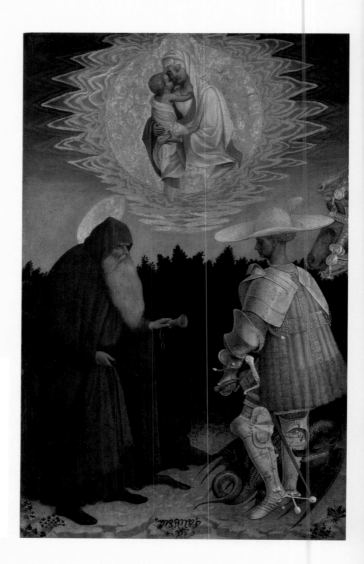

47. Pisanello, *The Virgin and Child with Saint George and Saint Anthony Abbot,* about 1435–41, egg tempera (nineteenth-century repaint) on poplar, 46.5 x 29 cm. This private devotional work is the artist's only signed painting and is generally thought to date from late in his career. Pisanello was chiefly famed as a medallist but he also painted on mural and panel.

CASE STUDY 2:
PICTURES REMADE TO SUIT CHANGING TASTE

Sassoferrato, *The Virgin and Child Embracing*, 1660–85
The Master of the Story of Griselda, *The Story of Patient Griselda: Part I (Marriage)*, about 1494

Documentary and technical evidence have uncovered two intriguing episodes during Eastlake's ambitious campaign of acquiring pictures from Italy in the 1850s and 1860s. Already the target of criticism for the cleaning of paintings at the Gallery, he seems to have taken steps to avoid controversy over Sassoferrato's *Virgin and Child Embracing* [48] that were not detected until the painting was cleaned again in 1986. During this treatment, the Virgin's blue robe and the green curtain were found to have been extensively overpainted.

A cross-section photograph taken from the robe [49] showed the original pale blue paint covered by later layers of varnish, a repaint of cobalt blue (not introduced to the artist's palette until the early nineteenth century) and a layer of brown toning. The explanation for these added layers is to be found in a memorandum from Eastlake to his Keeper of Paintings, Robert Wornum, dated 16 November 1864, which refers to the arrival of the painting from Venice where it had been bought: 'The Sasso Ferrato may be expected in a few weeks – it will, however, require a little

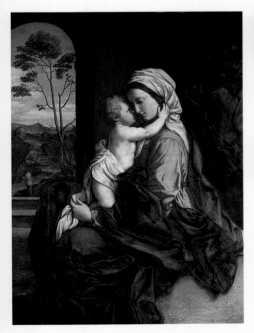

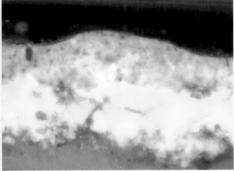

48. Sassoferrato, *The Virgin and Child Embracing*, 1660–85, oil on canvas, 97.2 × 74 cm, before cleaning. Sassoferrato modelled his work on the 'pure' style of an earlier age, much influenced by Raphael (page 49). He made his living painting devotional pictures using brilliant colours.

49. Cross-section from the Virgin's robe before cleaning, showing layers of repaint and toning.

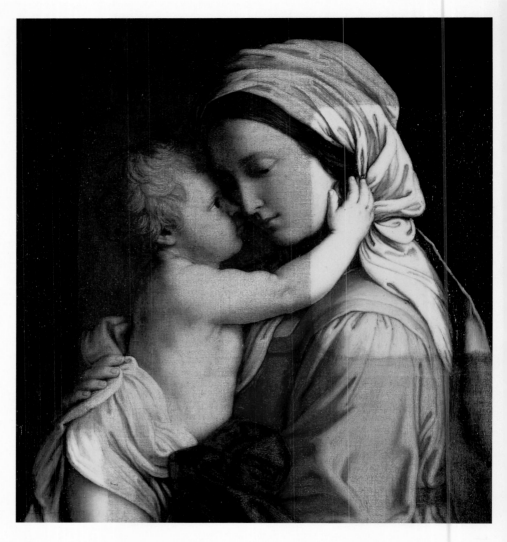

revision and possibly a little patina before it is put up.' In a later note, Eastlake mentions the visit of a restorer, Pinti, who was to varnish the picture only after it had been tried out in the gallery where it was to hang.

The brown toning found as one of the uppermost layers on the painting is undoubtedly Eastlake's 'patina' and the cobalt blue repaint is, presumably, the 'little revision' that he anticipated. In the 1986 cleaning they were removed [50],

revealing once more Sassoferrato's original colours [51]. So brilliant are they that it is not difficult to imagine Eastlake's nervousness at showing his new acquisition to a critical public and his instructions to Pinti to tone the painting down.

The cleaning of three panels illustrating the story of Patient Griselda, as told in Boccaccio's *Decameron*, demonstrates the extent to which paintings were sometimes altered by restorers. Among the episodes represented in the first

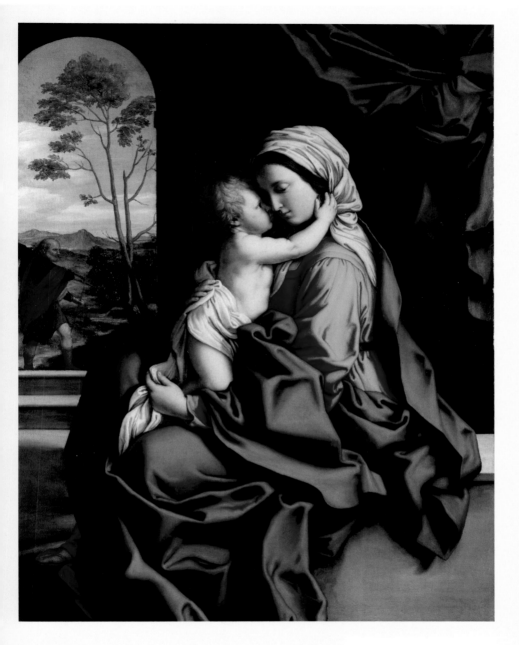

50. (Opposite) Detail of 48,
partly cleaned.

51. 48, after cleaning.

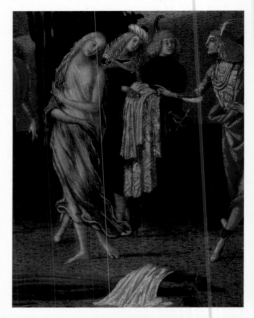

52. (Below) The Master of the Story of Griselda, *The Story of Patient Griselda, Part I*, about 1494, egg tempera and oil on wood, 61.6 × 154.3 cm. This anonymous painter takes his name from a series of three panels painted in Siena in the last decade of the fifteenth century and now in the collection of the National Gallery. This distinctive and decorative artist has not yet been identified.

53 and 54. These details show the figure of Griselda before cleaning and restoration, with her chemise (right), and after treatment in 2004 (opposite).

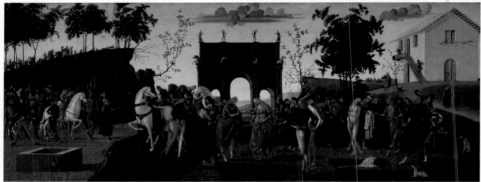

panel [52] is the initial trial of Griselda's patience, in which her bridegroom, the Marchese Gualtieri di Saluzzo, 'before the eyes of all his company ... caused her to be stripped naked' so that her simple peasant clothes (on the ground in front of her) could be replaced with the rich dress appropriate for his chosen bride (carried by the figure beside her). In 1874, when the National Gallery acquired the panels, it was felt that the artist's depiction of this episode was not suitable for public display and a restorer was asked to cover the naked figure with drapery [53]. He also repainted the position of her right arm and hand, presumably because the pose was thought to be indecorous.

When the painting was X-rayed, the original naked body was revealed to be underneath the later draperies. The overpainting was removed, restoring the original intention of both painter and writer. Moreover, the absurdity of Griselda with three, instead of two, sets of clothes is rectified [54].

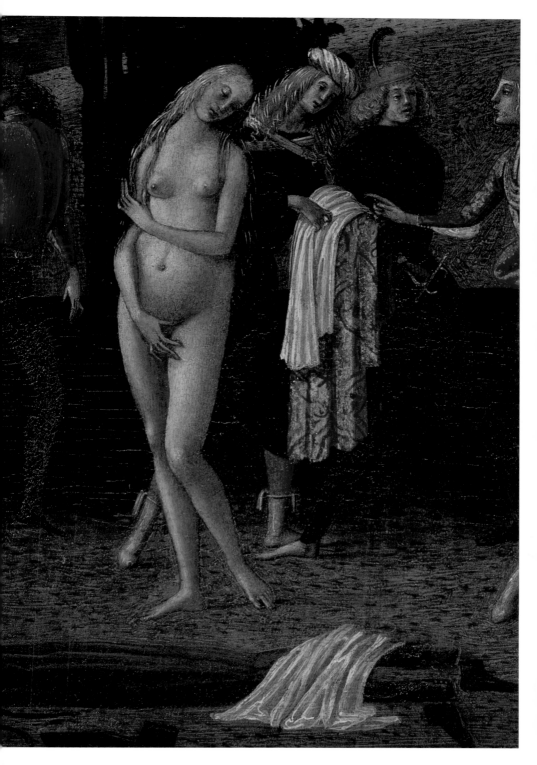

CASE STUDY 3:
IRREMOVABLE VARNISHES

George Stubbs, *A Gentleman driving a Lady in a Phaeton*, 1787
Hilaire-Germain-Edgar Degas, *Miss La La at the Cirque Fernando*, 1879

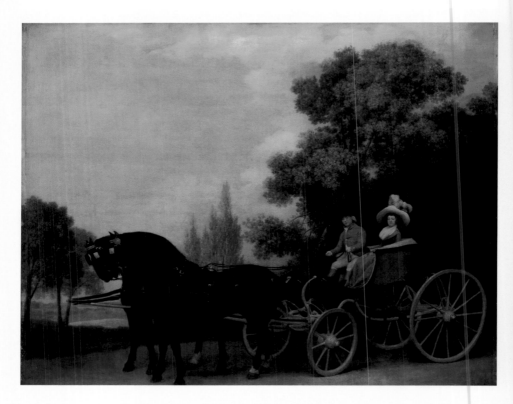

Neither of these paintings can be cleaned by traditional methods, despite the fact that they have discoloured varnishes that might, in other circumstances, be removed. The varnish on the Stubbs [52] is so yellowed that all the delicate handling of figures, trees and landscape is seen as if through a deep filter and many of the colour subtleties are concealed. The varnish on the Degas [53] is orange-yellow and quite darkened. Cleaning, one might think, would be highly desirable for both pictures – but it has been ruled out, because it cannot be accomplished without the danger of original material being removed.

Microchemical analysis has shown that Stubbs mixed a highly soluble stearine wax into the oil medium he used to paint this picture, presumably because it gave particular handling properties and soft, blurred paint textures that appealed to him. His panel paintings of this period are notorious for their experimental media and for the disasters that have befallen restorers who have tried to clean them.

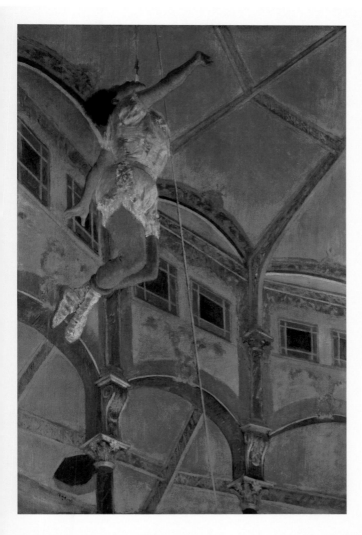

52. (Opposite) George Stubbs, *A Gentleman driving a Lady in a Phaeton*, 1787, oil and stearine wax on oak, 82.5 × 101.6 cm, detail.

53. Hilaire-Germain-Edgar Degas, *Miss La La at the Cirque Fernando*, 1879, oil on canvas, 117.2 × 77.5 cm.

Any solvent strong enough to dissolve the discoloured varnish will also dissolve the paint beneath it. Until scientific research can provide a varnish solvent specific enough to leave the stearine component intact, this particular cleaning will not be contemplated.

Cleaning was started on the Degas, to the extent of removing surface dirt, but was not pursued once a small sample of the varnish had been examined. It was found to contain orange pigment – the dominant colour of the painting itself. It was concluded that Degas (or somebody else) had brushed varnish on the painting before it was properly dry and that some of the orange paint had become incorporated into the varnish layer. Since the varnish contains original colouring matter, it cannot be removed.

The reasons are different – one because of the artist's chosen paint medium, the other probably a result of premature varnishing – but the result is the same: two paintings that will remain uncleaned.

CASE STUDY 4:
NO LINING, NO VARNISH

Vincent van Gogh, *A Wheatfield, with Cypresses*, 1889

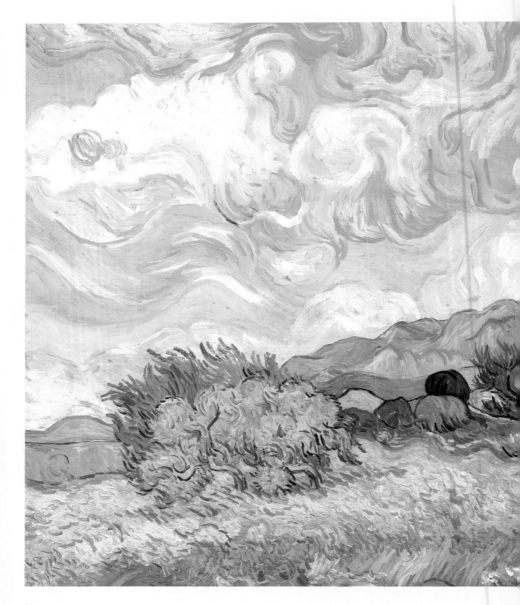

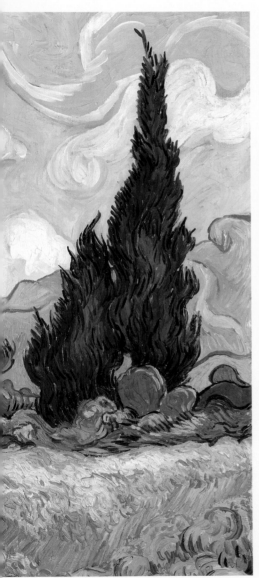

57. Vincent van Gogh, *A Wheatfield, with Cypresses*, 1889, oil on canvas, 72.1 × 90.9 cm. This painting was made at the mental asylum at St-Rémy, near Arles, where Van Gogh was a patient from May 1889 until May 1890.

Like many of Vincent van Gogh's paintings, *A Wheatfield, with Cypresses* [57] is fragile and vulnerable but, unusually, it has survived in almost perfect state. It has never been lined, consolidated or varnished – all processes that would have altered its original appearance irreversibly. Painted on exceptionally fine canvas with a thin lead-white ground, its technique is dramatically varied, as can be seen in a photograph taken with the light shining through the canvas [58]. Areas of bare, pale ground lie alongside massively thick brushstrokes – some of which have delicate, brittle points, while others bear the flattened impression of another canvas, presumably the result of being stacked behind and pressed against another painting when the paint was still wet. In other parts, there are thinner brushstrokes which, before examination and treatment in 1985–6, were beginning to curl and detach. The painting had also not been cleaned before that date and was covered in grey dirt. Traditional methods of consolidation for flaking paint were quite unacceptable in this case. In the past, lining or impregnation with adhesives would have been carried out which would have blackened the exposed canvas and ground and endangered the impasto. Unfortunately, many of Van Gogh's paintings have been lined – often using wax – and have darkened irretrievably. One example in the National Gallery Collection is *Van Gogh's Chair* in which the coarse canvas visible between the brushstrokes and around the edges – originally a pale buff colour – has become a deep brown, caused by saturation with wax [29].

The painting was first cleaned, removing the grey dirt with distilled water and a few drops of pure soap solution, applied in small amounts with soft brushes that did not catch the points of the impasto. The recovery of the original colours was dramatic [60]. The detaching paint was then treated on a specialised low-pressure suction table, developed in recent years at the National Gallery [59]. With highly controlled suction, warmth and humidity from the reverse, and the use of minute quantities of refined sturgeon's glue, this fragile painting was stabilised in an operation that would have been inconceivable a few years before. It has been left unvarnished, as close to its original appearance as possible. In order to protect the vulnerable surface, it is framed behind low-reflecting glass.

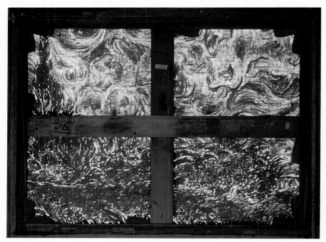

58. 57, photographed with transmitted light.

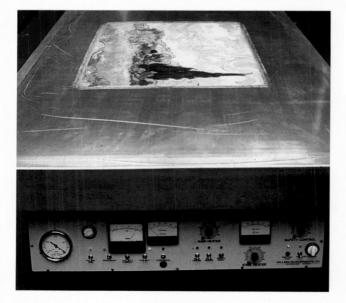

59. 57, on the suction table.

60. (Opposite) Detail of 57, showing a newly cleaned area, during treatment in 1985–6.

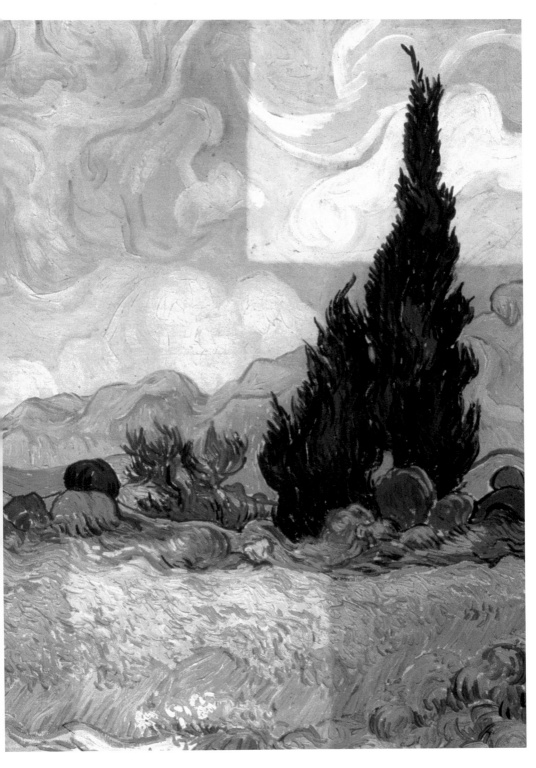

CASE STUDY 5:
A MAJOR RECONSTRUCTION

Giovanni Battista Cima da Conegliano, *The Incredulity of Saint Thomas*, about 1502–4

The treatment of Cima's altarpiece carried out during the 1970s and 1980s was a rare modern example of a process that was extensively practised (often unnecessarily) in the eighteenth and nineteenth centuries – the transfer of a painting to a new support. It is nowadays carried out only as a last resort, when all other attempts at treatment have proved unsuccessful.

The painting was commissioned in 1497 by the Scuola di San Tommaso dei Battuti for their altar in the church of San Francesco in Portogruaro, to the north of Venice, and was completed in 1504. From early in its history it seems to have suffered from flaking paint – partly, no doubt, through neglect, but probably also because of some fault in the preparation of the panel. This condition was considerably worsened when, while in the Accademia in Venice following restoration treatment in the early 1820s, it was submerged in the waters of the Grand Canal during a sudden flood tide.

It was bought by the National Gallery in 1870, by which time its state had become (according to Giovanni Morelli) 'deplorable', with large areas of loss and repaint. After its acquisition by the Gallery, deterioration continued, despite the repeated efforts of numerous restorers to treat it. Finally, in the 1950s, darkened, repainted and blistering all over [61], the panel was laid flat and paper facing stuck over the front to prevent any more paint being lost.

In the 1970s, further treatment and testing confirmed that adhesion between the ground and the panel had broken down irretrievably

in many places and that the panel itself was too rotten and worm-eaten in some parts to support the layers above. These observations led to the conclusion that the painting could only be saved by the complete removal of the original wood, followed by mounting on a new support.

The transfer of *The Incredulity of Saint Thomas* is simple to describe but was extraordinarily long, arduous and difficult to carry out. The painting was first freed of as much of its dark brown varnish and discoloured repaints as could be done safely, faced with layers of paper and fabric to protect the painted surface, and secured face-down. Then, in an operation lasting several years, the panel was gradually cut away from the back using sharp hand-held gouges [62]; in the final stages, as the reverse of the ground was being exposed, scalpels were used to pare away the last splinters of wood. It was at this point that the strong facing on the front became vital, because it was the only thing holding the delicate ground and paint layers together.

When all the wood had been removed, it was possible to consolidate the ground and paint from the reverse, prior to mounting them on a sheet of fine linen on a specially prepared synthetic panel. Finally, the layers of facing were taken off and the paint surface, now secure, could be seen for the first time since treatment had started. The remaining varnish and repaints were removed and the full extent of the damage sustained over the previous centuries was revealed [63], including countless needle holes where restorers had attempted to inject adhesives in the past [64]. The question now was how much the image, fragmented by

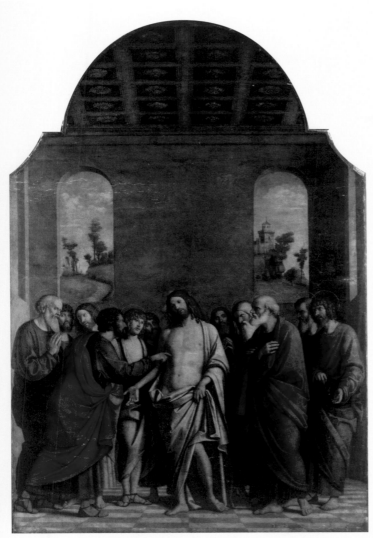

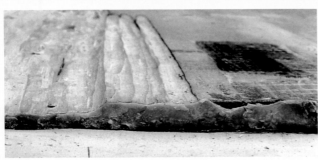

61. Giovanni Battista Cima da Conegliano, *The Incredulity of Saint Thomas*, about 1502–4, oil on synthetic panel, transferred from poplar, 294 × 199.4 cm. Before cleaning and reconstruction.

62. Removal of wooden panel.

widespread paint losses, should be reintegrated by inpainting.

In view of the illusionistic qualities intended for the altarpiece in its original setting, it was considered essential that the composition should be disrupted as little as possible. Therefore retouchings on the losses were matched as closely as possible to the original colours and forms, using the surviving paint in and around each damage as a guide. In parts that could not be reconstructed with certainty – for example, the embroidered pattern on the hem of Saint Thomas's green robe – retouching aimed at an unobtrusive rendering of form without finishing details.

The restored altarpiece [65] now hangs in the Sainsbury Wing at the end of the principal axis of the Gallery. The structural treatment and restoration that has enabled it to hang there in safety took more than 15 years to carry out.

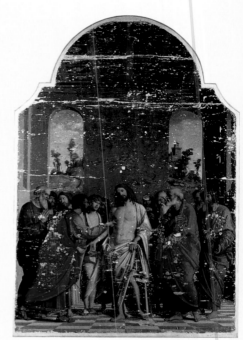

63. 61, after cleaning and reconstruction, before restoration.

64. Detail of a head in 61, with damages and needle holes, after cleaning and reconstruction, before restoration.

65. 61, after cleaning, reconstruction and restoration.

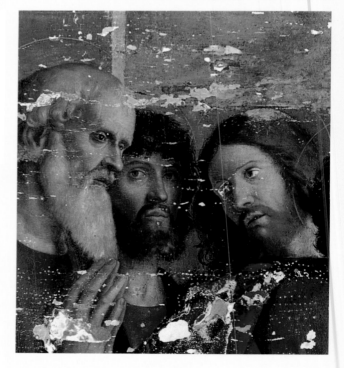

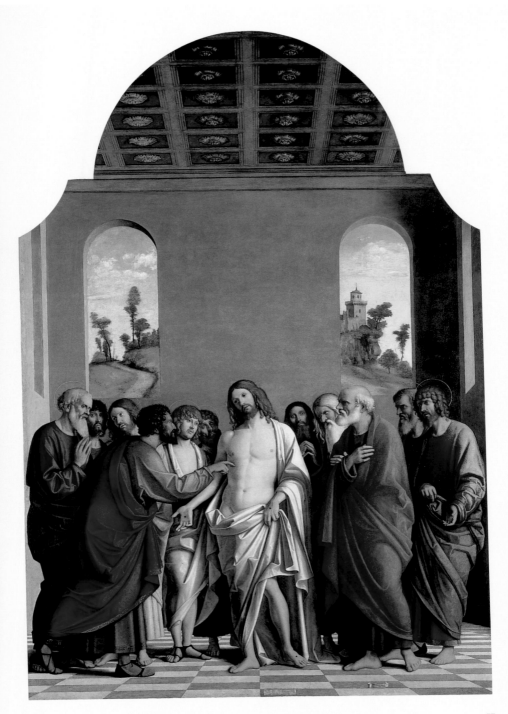

CASE STUDY 6:
THE PROBLEM OF OLD ADDITIONS

Follower of Campin, *The Virgin and Child before a Firescreen*, about 1440

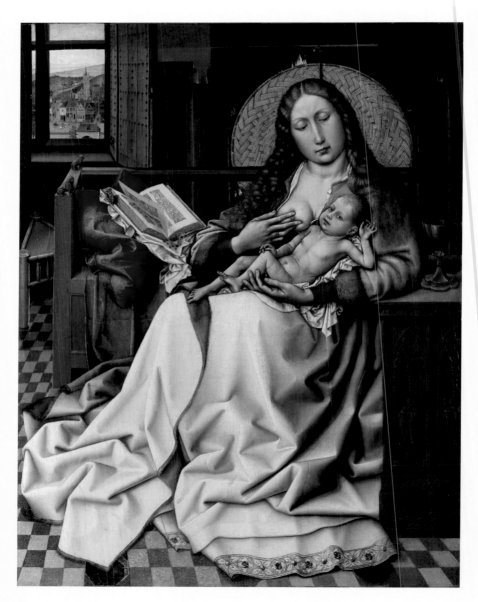

Nearly a quarter of this painting [66] is not original. A strip down the right side, which includes the cupboard and chalice, the Virgin's elbow and the right-hand parts of the firescreen and fireplace, was added in the nineteenth century. A narrower addition along the top, containing the upper part of the window with the horizontal window bar, the top of the shutter and parts of the fireplace, was made at the same time. Presumably, these additions replaced parts of the original panel that had been damaged (possibly in a fire) and cut away. However, it is unlikely that the nineteenth-century reconstructions of these parts are exact replicas of what was lost, since the structure of the top of the fireplace does not make sense and an old copy after this composition shows a much plainer cupboard and chalice than those now seen here.

When this picture was cleaned in 1992–3, a fundamental decision had to be made. Should the later parts be taken off and the panel exhibited as a fragment? Should they be kept and concealed in some way? Or should they be retained and left visible? In this case it was decided to preserve the well-known form of the composition in its entirety, including additions, but, in order to allow differentiation between original and later parts, the nineteenth-century paint was made fractionally different in tone at the retouching stage. A casual glance takes in the whole picture, but closer examination enables the additions to be distinguished.

This was a restoration dominated by the aesthetic problem of the additions, but the gain in visual clarity and the revelation of the quality of the original paint were the true reasons for cleaning. Hidden beneath more than a century of discoloured varnish and repaint were many telling details of great beauty – subtly coloured firelight catching the near edge of the window shutter and the leg of the stool, blazing points of the fire itself shining through the woven firescreen and tiny drops of milk on the Virgin's breast. Christ's genitals had also been painted out in a more prudish era [67] and were revealed by cleaning.

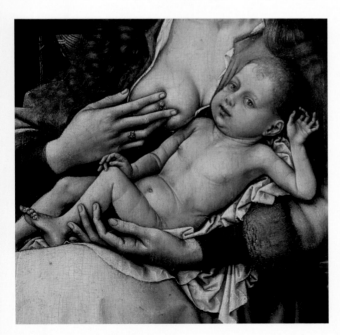

66. (Opposite) Follower of Robert Campin, *The Virgin and Child before a Firescreen*, about 1440, oil with egg tempera on oak with walnut additions, 63.4 × 48.5 cm.

67. (Left) Detail of Christ Child in 66, before 1992–3 cleaning.

CASE STUDY 7:
STRATEGIES OF RETOUCHING

Duccio, Three panels from the 'Maestà', 1311

These panels all come from Duccio's gigantic
double-sided altarpiece, which was carried in
triumph from Duccio's workshop to be placed
on the high altar of Siena Cathedral in 1311.
The Annunciation was originally part of the
front predella (the base of the altarpiece), while
Jesus opens the Eyes of a Man born Blind and
The Transfiguration were from the back predella.
The altarpiece was removed from the high altar
in 1506 and eventually sawn into pieces in 1771.
The main sections are still in Siena but some
of the individual scenes from the front predella
and most of those from the back predella were
dispersed into collections throughout the world.
These three found their separate ways into the
National Gallery Collection at the end of the
nineteenth century.

They are, in general, well-preserved, but each
of them has specific areas of paint loss that have
been retouched in different ways. In each case,
some form of visible inpainting has been chosen
instead of fully matched deceptive retouching.
The Annunciation [68] has lost paint in areas
along the bottom and left sides. At the bottom
it is inpainted with a plain grey and at the side
the gilding has been imitated in yellow–orange

68. Duccio, *The Annunciation*, 1311, egg tempera
on poplar, 43 × 44 cm. Duccio was one of
the most esteemed and influential painters of
the fourteenth century in Italy. He worked mainly
in his native Siena. This panel was the first scene
on the front predella of the 'Maestà', a large
double-sided altarpiece which was installed in
the Duomo, the cathedral in Siena, in 1311.

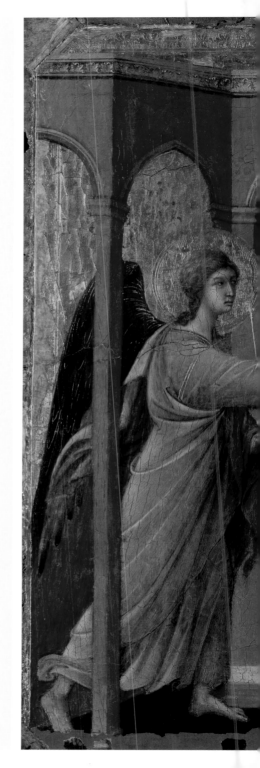

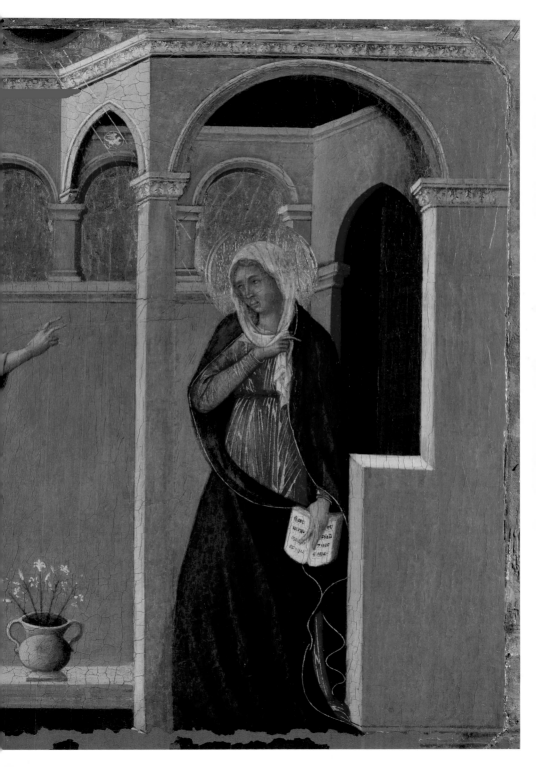

paint. No attempt has been made to reconstruct the missing forms.

On *The Transfiguration* [69] the entire upper body of Saint John is lost together with some of the adjacent background. Here the loss has been filled with a pale brown tone and the probable form of the figure has been indicated with drawing lines by the restorer. In addition, the level of the filling in the loss has been left at a slightly lower level than that of the surrounding original paint.

The single major area of damage on *Jesus opens the Eyes of a Man born Blind* [70] is a most crucial one. By cruel irony it occurs at the focus of the entire episode: the face of the cured blind man at the right has flaked away [70]. Here, a more or less deceptive reconstruction was essential in order not to disrupt the narrative power of the scene. Happily, the blind man was depicted twice by Duccio and the face was therefore copied from the same figure shown in the middle of the panel at an earlier stage in the story. However, in order to indicate that this is not original paint, the prominent craquelure visible elsewhere on the picture has not been imitated.

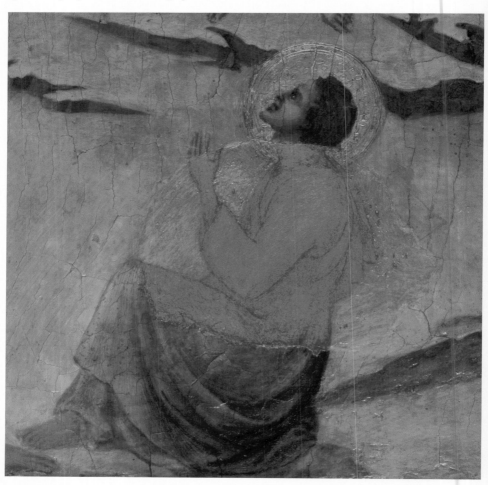

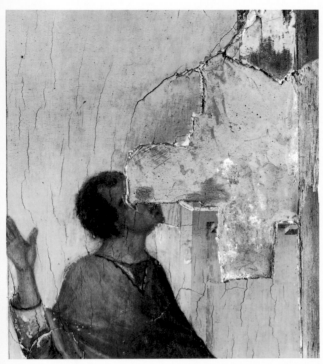

69. (Opposite) Duccio, *The Transfiguration*, 1311, egg tempera on poplar, 44 × 46 cm, detail.

70. Duccio, *Jesus opens the Eyes of a Man born Blind*, 1311, egg tempera on poplar, 43.5 × 45 cm, after cleaning, detail.

71. (Below) Detail of 70, after cleaning and restoration.

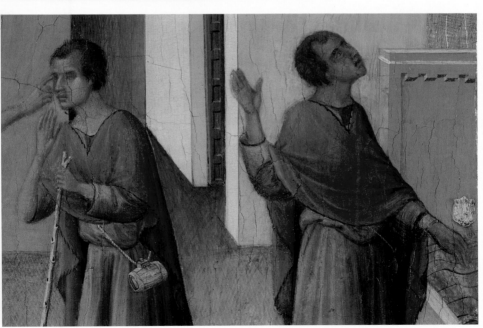

CASE STUDY 8:
RESTORING A MUCH-LOVED MASTERPIECE

Hans Holbein the Younger, *Jean de Dinteville and Georges de Selve ('The Ambassadors')*, 1533

Hans Holbein's full-length double portrait of two French diplomats, painted in London in 1533, is one of the great masterpieces of Renaissance portraiture.

The sitters are Jean de Dinteville and Georges de Selve. The portrait was presumably commissioned by the former, as it was in the Dinteville family château in Champagne that the portrait afterwards hung. Dinteville was in England as ambassador from the court of France. Georges de Selve, Bishop of Lavaur, appears to have visited him in the spring of 1533.

The greatest curiosity of the painting is the anamorphosis, or distortion, of a skull, which is only clearly seen as such when standing at an angle to the right of the picture, or when looking through a cylindrical piece of glass. This is almost certainly a reference to the sitters' own mortality, despite the richness of their appearance. In the top left-hand corner, just visible behind the green curtain, is a crucifix, a reminder of the Christian promise of salvation.

In 1992 the National Gallery decided to undertake the conservation of Holbein's *'Ambassadors'*. Even before the picture was acquired in 1890 it had suffered considerably [72]. Holbein used a very large panel, made up of ten oak planks, which had expanded and contracted over the years, in response to changes in temperature and humidity; this movement had damaged the paint along the joins. At some point, the picture had also suffered water damage, which affected the paint along the lower edge and on the left-hand side. Earlier attempts to repair the damaged areas meant that the cumulative effect of these now-discoloured

fillings and retouchings was to cover much well-preserved original paint; together with dirt and cloudy varnish, these had considerably obscured Holbein's painting.

The right-hand part of the painting, with the figure of Georges de Selve, is very well preserved indeed. The left-hand side of the picture has suffered the most. The figure of Jean de Dinteville has two large losses in the central part of his body, and it was decided to leave old areas of restoration in place here. On his chest Dinteville wears the medallion of the Order of Saint Michael, the French equivalent of the English Order of the Garter. The present medallion is entirely old restoration, as the X-radiograph of this area clearly shows, although it presumably closely imitates what Holbein originally painted; most of the chain from which it hangs is Holbein's work. Another old restoration has been retained is the area where Dinteville would have worn a codpiece, now composed of largely undifferentiated black paint. Some of the folds of his lower garment, painted by Holbein as arranged around the codpiece, but obscured by earlier restoration, are now visible again.

In the central section of the painting the objects on the shelves are less damaged, but the skull, lower down, had not only lost much original paint but had also suffered further from earlier restoration attempts [73]. Most of the original paint of the middle and lower end of the skull was overpainted so that the illusion of the distorted skull had ceased to make sense; the nose bone was particularly unconvincing. Computerised distortions based on photographs of a real skull were made by the National

72. Hans Holbein the Younger, *Jean de Dinteville and Georges de Selve ('The Ambassadors')*, 1533, oil on oak, 207 × 209.5 cm, before cleaning. Holbein spent two periods working in England, primarily in the court of Henry VIII. This portrait was produced during his second stay, which lasted from 1532 until his death, probably from the plague, in 1543.

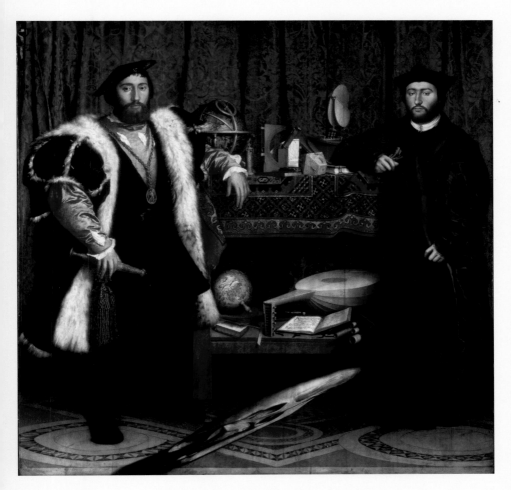

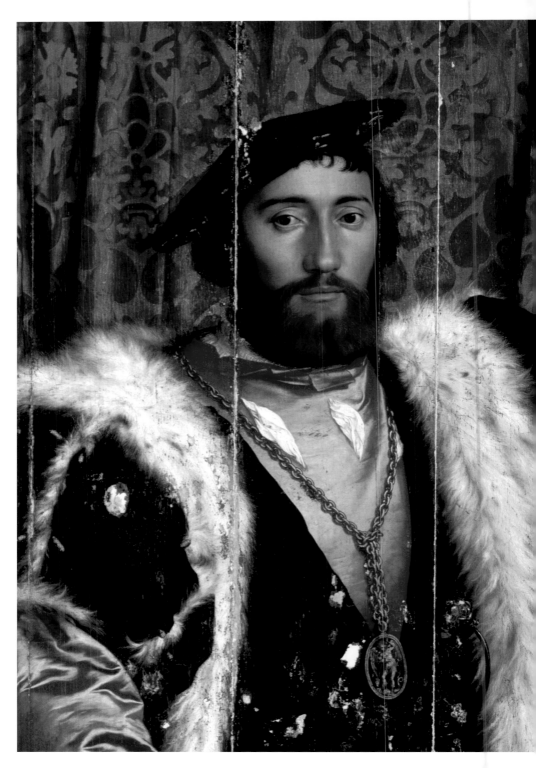

Gallery's scientific department, and helped to show the shape of the nose bone as it must originally have been painted. Together with the careful recovery of areas of Holbein's original paint, it was possible to attempt a reconstruction of the skull and bring it closer to what the artist must have painted.

Cleaning, restoring and reframing the picture took over three years, and we can now appreciate the achievement of this great portrait once more. Holbein's signature is now clearly legible on the lower left-hand side. The lute-case which lies on the floor under the shelves was uncovered and many details of Jean de Dinteville's black costume are now clear, as are the marvellous contrasts of different textures of fabrics – silk, satin and velvet – so characteristic of Holbein. The picture is also revealed as exceptionally colourful, highlighting contrasts between Dinteville's pink satin sleeve and the turquoise blue of the astronomical globe and between the predominant red of the table carpet and the green damask curtain [74].

73. Detail of 72, after cleaning, before restoration.

74. (Below) 72, after cleaning and restoration.

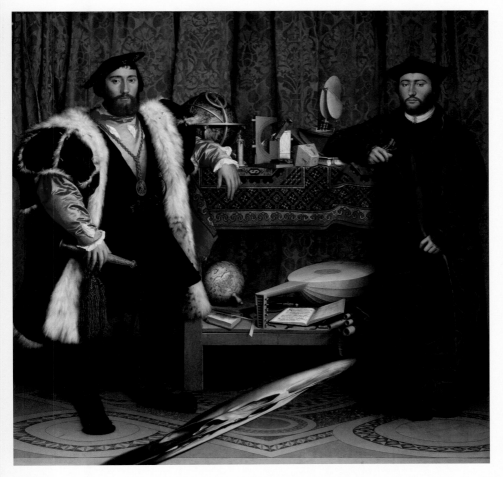

CASE STUDY 9:
REASSEMBLING THE FRAGMENTS

Francesco Pesellino, *The Pistoia Santa Trinità Altarpiece,* 1455–60

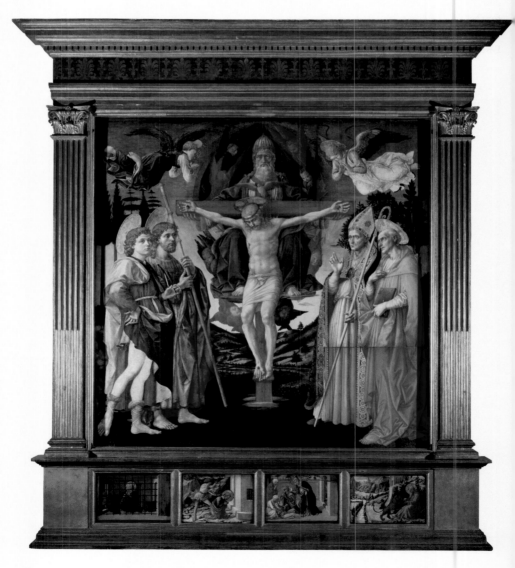

A bizarre history of dismemberment for predatory collectors, followed by later recovery and reassembly is apparent on even the most casual examination of this altarpiece. The *Pistoia Santa Trinità* altarpiece [75] was begun by Francesco Pesellino and finished after his death in 1457 by Fra Filippo Lippi who delivered it in 1460. There is a fascinating set of documents describing the commissioning of the altarpiece for the Compagnia dei Preti in Pistoia and what happened to it when left uncompleted on Pesellino's death. It was taken from Florence to

75. (Opposite) Francesco Pesellino, completed by Fra Filippo Lippi and workshop, *The Pistoia Santa Trinità Altarpiece*, 1455–60, egg tempera and oil on wood, about 185.5 × 181 cm. Francesco di Stefano was brought up by his painter grandfather Pesello, after whom he was nicknamed 'Pesellino' ('little Pesello'). Pesellino died suddenly, while still a young man, hence the completion of this, his only surviving documented work, by Fra Filippo Lippi.

76. 75, as it was in about 1923.

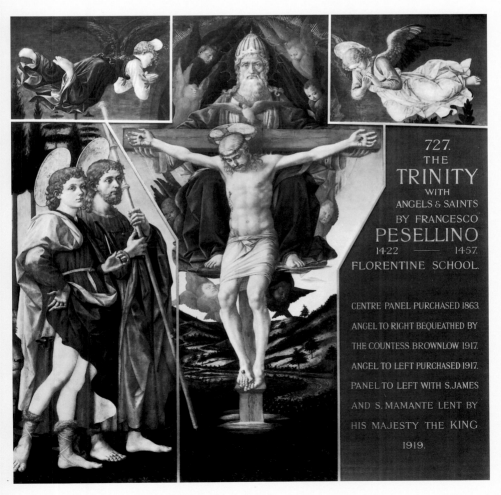

727.
THE
TRINITY
WITH
ANGELS & SAINTS
BY FRANCESCO
PESELLINO
1422 ———— 1457.
FLORENTINE SCHOOL.

CENTRE PANEL PURCHASED 1863.
ANGEL TO RIGHT BEQUEATHED BY
THE COUNTESS BROWNLOW 1917.
ANGEL TO LEFT PURCHASED 1917.
PANEL TO LEFT WITH S.JAMES
AND S. MAMANTE LENT BY
HIS MAJESTY THE KING
1919.

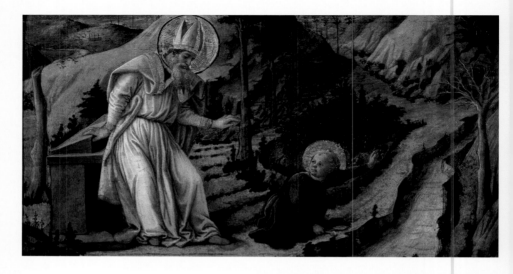

77. Fra Filippo Lippi, *The Vision of Saint Augustine*,
1455–60, tempera on wood, 28 × 511.5 cm.
The State Hermitage Museum, St Petersburg.

Prato for Filippo Lippi to complete, having been assessed by Lippi and Domenico Veneziano as just half-finished. Meanwhile, a financial dispute was in progress between Pesellino's widow and his business partner, which complicated the final payments made to her for her husband's work on the painting. How much was painted by Pesellino and how much by Lippi was the subject of disagreement then and has been ever since. The altarpiece was removed from its church in Pistoia in the eighteenth century and, presumably at that time, the main panel was sawn into five fragments – which, apart from the two angels, one might imagine to be so irregular in shape as to make them unsaleable. Nevertheless they were sold and dispersed.

The *Crucifixion* fragment was purchased in 1863 by the National Gallery. It was clear that it was part of a larger panel and so the hunt was on for the other pieces. Three other fragments were found over the next 65 years. Unfortunately, the fourth (depicting the two saints at the left) was already in the Royal

Collection and not for sale: it was, however, placed on permanent loan to the Gallery and was reunited with the other parts in 1919 [76]. The bottom part of the right-hand pair of saints, who were discovered in 1929, was never found and a restorer was commissioned to paint their lower robes and feet.

The predella panels (see p.88), also sawn apart in the eighteenth century, were bequeathed in 1937. But the final piece of the jigsaw was discovered only in 1995, 132 years after the reassembly began. The predella, now assumed to be entirely by Lippi and his workshop rather than by Pesellino, had always appeared too short for the main panel and any frame it may have had originally. But then the missing centre part of the predella was identified – a panel by Lippi, *The Vision of Saint Augustine*, now in the Hermitage, Saint Petersburg [77]. Scholars knew it existed – some had even remarked on its affinities with the *Pistoia Santa Trinità* altarpiece – but nobody had suggested that it was part of the very same plank as the other predella panels.

CASE STUDY 10:
A 'FAMOUS' PAINTING UNCOVERED

Jan Gossaert, *The Virgin and Child*, 1527

In 1860 a small arch-topped panel showing the Virgin and Child seated in a stone niche [78] was acquired by the National Gallery as one of 46 paintings from the Paris collection of Edmund Beaucousin. It was immediately sent to Dublin as 'superfluous' to the collection at Trafalgar Square. In 1926 it returned to London but remained in obscurity, considered to be no more than one of several copies of a lost painting by Jan Gossaert, the celebrated painter who worked for the courts of the Low Countries and Denmark in the first part of the sixteenth century. Gossaert's composition was regarded as sufficiently famous to be engraved in 1589 ('insignis' in the inscription), but strangely none of the known copies, including the

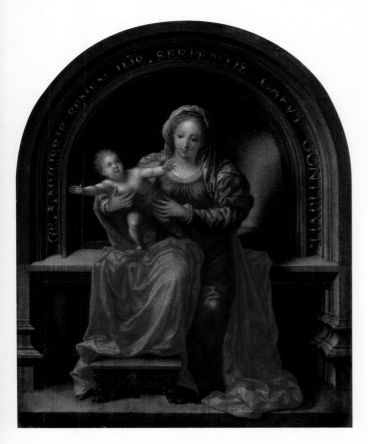

78. Jan Gossaert, *The Virgin and Child*, 1527, oil on oak, 30.5 × 23.5 cm, before cleaning and restoration. Gossaert worked for the courts of the Low Countries and Denmark in the first part of the sixteenth century. This hidden masterpiece, obscured under layers of repainting, was thought to be a copy painted in the seventeenth or eighteenth centuries until it was X-rayed and cleaned at the National Gallery.

National Gallery version, matched precisely the figures in the engraving. Moreover, as well as a much darkened varnish, this panel had a cracked and wrinkled surface quite unlike that usually seen on a sixteenth-century panel. It is not surprising that it was assumed to be a late copy.

When the panel was X-rayed, however, it became apparent that in certain details the image revealed [80] was closer to that of the engraving than the visible painted surface: for example, the fingers of the Child's outstretched arm are straight in the painting and curled in the print and the X-ray image, while the Virgin's white veil extends across her shoulder to the Child's head in the print and X-ray but not in the painting. In addition, the oak panel appeared to be old and when the wood was analysed by dendrochronology (tree-ring dating) it was found to date from the early sixteenth century. The pigments and layer structure revealed by

two tiny paint samples also supported the likelihood that the painting was made in Gossaert's lifetime but had been altered by later repainting.

Removal of the repainting and the exceptionally thick discoloured varnish – which turned out to have wrinkled as a result of the addition of too much oil – revealed a design exactly as in the engraving and a work of such quality and refinement of execution that it could only be by Gossaert [81]. Since the panel is generally very well preserved, it seems that the overpainting that disguised its identity was carried out for reasons of taste. For instance, in addition to reducing the Virgin's shoulders and jawline, the earlier restorer widened her mouth, giving her a sweeter expression not unlike that of Virgins in paintings by Correggio, greatly admired in the eighteenth and nineteenth centuries.

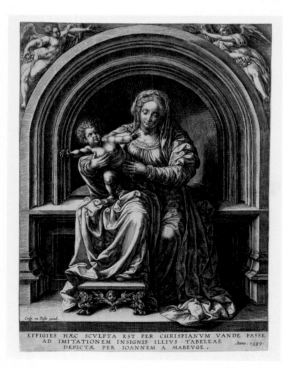

EFFIGIES HÆC SCVLPTA EST PER CHRISPIANVM VANDE PASSE
AD IMITATIONEM INSIGNIS ILLIVS TABELLAE
DEPICTÆ PER IOANNEM A MABEVGE.

79. Crispijn de Passe the Elder, engraving of *The Virgin and Child*, dated 1589.

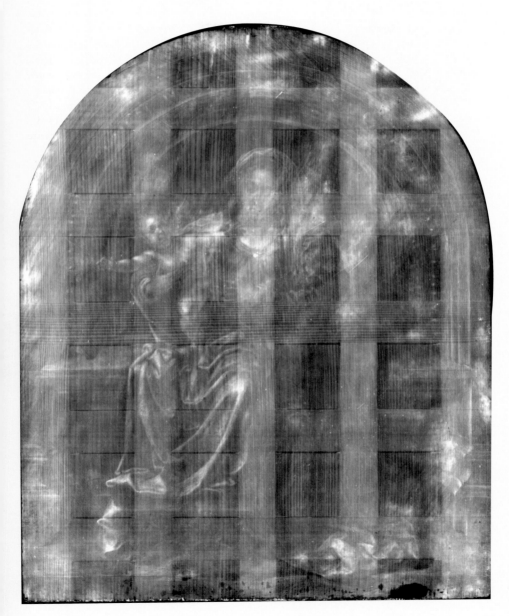

80. An X-ray of *The Virgin and Child*

81. 78, after cleaning
and restoration.

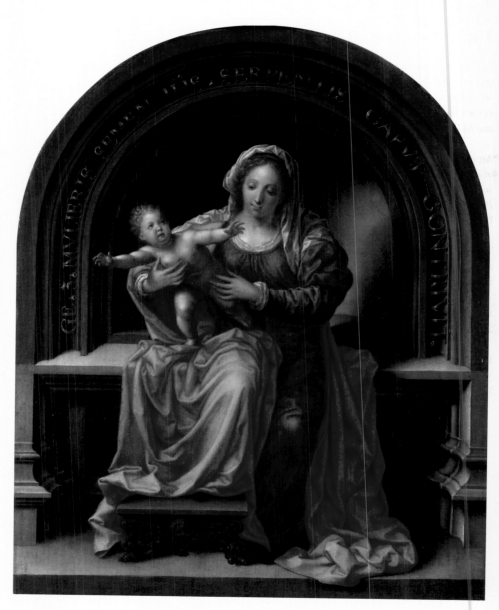

FIND OUT MORE

The most comprehensive and extensively illustrated book on the processes of conservation and restoration is: K. Nicolaus, *The Restoration of Paintings*, Cologne 1999.

Important historical texts on the philosophy and practice of conservation and restoration are collected in: *Readings in Conservation: Issues in the Conservation of Paintings*, eds D. Bomford and M. Leonard, Los Angeles 2004.

An exceptionally useful handbook on the study of easel paintings as physical objects is: A. Kirsh and R.S. Levenson, *Seeing Through Paintings: Physical Examination in Art Historical Studies*, New Haven and London 2000.

The following publications discuss various aspects of the structure and care of paintings in the National Gallery Collection.

D. Bomford, J. Kirby, J. Leighton and A. Roy, *Art in the Making: Impressionism*, London 1990.

D. Bomford (ed.), Art in the Making: *Underdrawings in Renaissance Paintings*, London 2002.

D. Bomford, S. Herring, J. Kirby, C. Riopelle and A. Roy, *Art in the Making: Degas*, London 2004.

D. Bomford, J. Kirby, A. Roy, A. Rüger and R. White, *Art in the Making: Rembrandt*, London 2006.

J. Dunkerton, S. Foister and N. Penny, *Dürer to Veronese: Sixteenth-Century Painting in The National Gallery*, London and New Haven 1999.

S. Foister, A. Roy and M. Wyld, *Making and Meaning: Holbein's Ambassadors*, London 1997.

D. Gordon, *Making and Meaning: The Wilton Diptych*, London 1993.

Articles on the conservation, restoration and technical study of paintings in the National Gallery Collection are published annually in *The National Gallery Technical Bulletin*.

ENJOY MORE NATIONAL GALLERY BOOKS

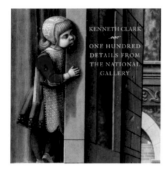 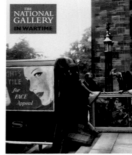 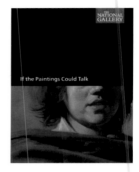

One Hundred Details from the National Gallery
Kenneth Clark

This magnificent re-issue of the landmark title contains stunning details from favourite paintings in the National Gallery's collection.

The National Gallery in Wartime
Suzanne Bosman

This richly illustrated book brings together previously unseen material from the National Gallery's archive.

If the Paintings Could Talk …
Michael Wilson

A fascinating miscellany of facts, quotations and tales creates an alternative tour of the great art and artists in the National Gallery. Preface by broadcaster Andrew Marr.

FSC
Mixed Sources
Product group from well-managed
forests and other controlled sources

Cert no. SGS-COC-002987
www.fsc.org
© 1996 Forest Stewardship Council

National Gallery publications generate valuable revenue for the Gallery, to ensure that future generations are able to enjoy the paintings as we do today. For our latest titles and special offers, visit our online shop **www.nationalgallery.co.uk/shop**.

All photography © The National Gallery, London except: Amsterdam: © Rijksmuseum, Amsterdam, fig. 79; London: © Getty Images, fig. 5; St Petersburg: State Hermitage Museum © akg-images, fig. 77